"Tim Kelley gives us all a road map for the discovery of our true purpose in life. No other book that I have ever come across lays out the journey in such a thoughtful, challenging, and motivating way. If you want a life filled with meaning and purpose, let Tim be your guide. You won't be disappointed!"

–**HOWARD BEHAR,** Former president of Starbucks Coffee

"Tim Kelley's work is of the highest caliber. His insight, precision, and skill shine out from a field that is typically hazy. If you are called to explore the realm of purpose, I know of no better guide than Tim."

–**HELEN PALMER,** Best-selling author of *The Enneagram*

"What Einstein did for physics and Gutenberg did for printing, *True Purpose* does for purpose. You'll discover that we've been in nursery school with respect to what we know and how we access purpose. This book puts us into college. Whether you know your purpose or not, I urge you to read this book and do its exercises. It will put you on a path of magic and blessings. *True Purpose* will be the standard for years to come. Well done, Tim."

–**MARTIN RUTTE,** Co-editor of *Chicken Soup for the Soul at Work*
Founder of www.ProjectHeavenOnEarth.com

"*True Purpose* is a profound book that walks you through a step-by-step, proven process to discover your life's purpose. Tim is a master, and I have personally watched him transform hundreds of people's lives—including my own."

–**MARCIA WIEDER,** Founder & CEO of Dream University®
Author of *Making Your Dreams Come True*

"Tim Kelley understands human nature—on the ground level and according to our highest desires. Any person who desires to make an ongoing impact with their work and life will benefit from the ideas and steps he shares in this book. At once practical and wise, *True Purpose* will give you a broader and deeper understanding of your motivations and the actions that will move you in powerful new directions toward the greatest challenges that are still ahead of you."

–**JOHN MITCHELL,** Former president of Planters & LifeSavers Co., and
Former president of Business Printer Division, Lexmark International, Inc.

"*True Purpose* offers practical strategies to help meet one of life's greatest challenges: finding our unique path and giving our life true meaning. Tim Kelley's methods draw on his own inner work, his extensive coaching experience, his passion, and his creative gifts. This is a highly original and useful book."

–**RIANE EISLER,** Author of *The Chalice and the Blade*,
The Real Wealth of Nations, and *The Power of Partnership*

"Tim Kelley has pioneered a methodology which will allow you to understand your very specific purpose and begin to find the satisfaction that comes when one's life activity is centered on that purpose. Tim's new book, *True Purpose,* embodies the knowledge and experience he has gained in this life's work, complete with exercises and clear instructions as to how we can bring this understanding into each of our daily lives."

–**SIMON RICH, Jr.,** Former Chairman & CEO of Louis Dreyfus
Natural Gas, and Chairman of the Board of Visitors at Nicholas School
of the Environment and Earth Sciences, Duke University

"Knowing your *real* purpose is essential to doing big things in the world. Tim's book will help you find your true purpose—and start living it."

–**MICHAEL PORT,** Author of *The Think Big Manifesto*
and *Book Yourself Solid*

True Purpose

True Purpose

12 Strategies for Discovering the Difference You Are Meant to Make

Tim Kelley

TRANSCENDENT® SOLUTIONS PRESS

Berkeley, California

For information, contact the publisher:

Transcendent Solutions Press
info@transcendentsolutionspress.com

Printed in the United States of America on acid-free paper.

Publisher's Cataloging-in-Publication Data

Kelley, Tim (Timothy A.), 1962-

True purpose : 12 strategies for discovering the difference you are meant to make / Tim Kelley.

p. ; cm.

Includes index.

ISBN: 978-0-615-26793-7

1. Self-actualization (Psychology) 2. Personal coaching. 3. Conduct of life. I. Title.

BF637.S4 K45 2009

158.1   2009900080

Book Producer: Brookes Nohlgren | www.BooksByBrookes.com
Book Designer: Peri Poloni-Gabriel | www.KnockoutBooks.com
Editor: Jennifer Repo | www.TheBookBistro.com
Indexer: Bruce Tracy, Ph.D. | indexer@lightspeed.net

For my wife, Heather, and my son, Ronan,

who give me purpose

Contents

Acknowledgments

First and foremost, I thank my good friend Marcia Wieder. It was in Marcia's Dream Coach® Certification program that I first became really clear about my life's purpose. Not only have Marcia and her programs been a support to me, but she referred many of my early clients, encouraged me to become a public speaker, and provided me with some of my first speaking venues.

I also thank Ann McIndoo for helping me get this book out of my head and onto paper. Her process was extraordinary and helped me to write a book in far less time than I ever imagined possible.

Many teachers helped me learn the methods that I'm sharing with you in this book. Foremost among them are Carole Kammen, Jodi Gold, and Lynnea Lumbard, who brought me from the technical world into the spiritual one and showed me how the psyche works. I owe all of them a great debt of gratitude for preparing me to be a vehicle for my purpose.

Creating this book was quite an endeavor, and I am deeply indebted to my crack team of editors, designers and marketers: Elizabeth Marshall, Brookes Nohlgren, Jennifer Repo, Janet Goldstein, and Peri Gabriel. Thank you all for helping me get my message out to the world.

I offer special thanks to all of the clients, coaches, and workshop participants who very generously allowed me to use their personal communications with their souls and egos as examples. Your willingness to share your own stories and messages will greatly contribute to many others finding their purpose. Thank you.

I also thank my lovely wife, Heather, and my son, Ronan, for their patience with me during the time of transition from doing technical work to becoming an author, speaker, executive coach, and consultant. Your faith and support have made me the man I am.

Foreword

Marcia Wieder,

Founder & CEO of Dream University®

True Purpose is a profound book that walks you through a step-by-step, proven process to discover your life's purpose. When you are living on purpose, your intentions, your goals, and the quality of your dreams will change. And, if you are ready, so will your life. If you're not ready or if you're unsure, this book will help you to prepare.

As the Founder & CEO of Dream University® and creator of the Dream Coach® methodology, I've been speaking, writing, and teaching about finding your life's purpose and dreams for close to 20 years. Early in life, I was grateful to discover that my purpose was "to inspire." I remember the day I realized it, feeling joyful and alive. It was a gift to know what really mattered to me and to discover what my life would be dedicated to. From that place, I wrote four books on the subject and have impacted hundreds of thousands of people, millions if you count my *Oprah* appearances. Many people consider me a respected resource and a thought leader on this topic.

So imagine my surprise when Tim Kelley personally took me through his process and my purpose changed. I found a deeper cut and more truthful expression of who I am and why I am here. Now I would say that my purpose is "To believe." Sounds simple, right?

With this knowledge, my life changed. Not drastically or overnight, but subtly, and over time, profoundly. With greater insight and understanding about what was unconsciously running my life, I was able to make critical shifts that put my soul at the helm. Knowing my purpose continues to bring clarity about both what I want and don't want. I've developed the practice of saying "No thank you" or "No more"; I now have more energy and resources to say "Yes" to dreams that are the expression of my true nature. And as I release what is no longer true for me, or is out of integrity with my soul, I have more time and freedom for what resonates with my heart. My work and message changed, and as I deepened, my credibility increased. I now make decisions in alignment with my purpose and am rewarded with both peace and abundance. Family, friends, and clients continue to comment on the difference they see in me. I am living a richer, more fulfilling life. This is what's possible for you by reading this book.

I've known Tim both personally and professionally for many years. Educated at MIT, serving as an officer in the U.S. Navy, and working at Oracle Corporation: such diversity created a unique man. Being a seeker in his own right led him to become a spiritual teacher, leader, and workshop conductor. Tim is a powerful blend of head and heart, compassion and relentless truth-telling.

Tim has taught his masterful process for several years to hundreds of Certified Dream Coaches. Many have invested wisely to return and attend the advanced Dream Coach Group Leader program that he leads. As a speaker and published author, his message has impacted global audiences and leaders from all walks of life. All that he has accomplished and created were part of a divine plan initiated by his soul. He was groomed to create a unique body of work and became masterful at helping people find their purpose and to live as the highest and most honest expression of their soul. Over the years, in watching Tim practice what he preaches, I have witnessed him decline offers and opportunities that were not congruent with his soul's work. I've seen him take risks that only someone who trusts himself can take. Without sounding trite, he walks his talk, which has often inspired me to do the same. What he has created is distinctive, powerful, and accessible. If you do the exercises he has provided, you too will discover or deepen your relationship to your soul: a place of great wisdom, clarity, and, most importantly, faith.

Similar to some books on this topic, you will be supported in finding your life's purpose. But quite different from any other process, you will go deep inside yourself to find the answers. And you won't be left there. You will clearly understand what it takes to make this critical knowledge stick. And most importantly, the source for this knowing will be your soul. When it comes to hearing from your own trusted source (a compelling tool you will learn), it doesn't get any better than utilizing Tim's methods. Imagine knowing who you are, so you can better understand what you want and then have greater courage to act on it.

Many of the critical points introduced, such as creating the "right relationship" between your ego and soul, are so essential that it's hard to imagine anyone writing an effective book on this topic excluding them. Without this skill, I've seen many fail, falter, and suffer unnecessarily. As you learn to use your ego in partnership with your soul, you will experience less conflict and self-sabotaging behaviors. As Tim explains, we need to honor our soul and ego and develop the ability to literally hear from them both. Navigating this critical relationship is a level of mastery that some people pay thousands of dollars to understand and be guided through. This same process that you are now holding in your hand can deepen your connection to your soul, allowing for great insight. You don't need to go to someone else to peek into the depth of your being because who you truly are will be revealed to you.

Here is a specific example of a life-altering insight I culled from *True Purpose*. I learned to slow down the negative inner dialogue in my head by assigning a new "job description" to a self-destructive part that often undermined my creative ideas. Specifically, my internal critic was harsh and debilitating, so I gave it a new assignment as a "coach." Now, when I try something new or take a risk, it first offers validating feedback and, then, constructive feedback. I am more forgiving, compassionate, and confident to dream bigger dreams. How much happier would you be if you could quiet your inner critic?

Here are a few more questions for you to consider. When the proverbial end comes, how do you want to feel about the life you've lived? How would you change your life if you knew with certainty that the path you are on is the right one? What choices or decisions would you make today armed with greater clarity? As I stated earlier, standing in your purpose, the quality of your life will change. Now all you need to do is find your *True Purpose*. This is what living a dream-come-true life is really about.

If your life is mostly about safety, security, or maintaining the status quo, you could find your *True Purpose* and choose to change nothing, or perhaps even choose not to know. But I assume since you are reading this important book, that's not who you are. There are both opportunities and responsibilities that come with this knowing. Yet, if you are committed to awakening and living into your destiny, what choice do you really have?

You have made a priceless investment in the future of your own life, and since it's never been a more important time to pursue your dreams, don't lose another day not knowing who you really are and what you truly want. Live the life you were born and destined to live. We never know when the end will come, and for most of us, whenever it arrives, it will be too soon. That's why you must live every day as the gift it is and each moment as precious. If you truly want to say that you lived your life, then it's time to find your *True Purpose*.

Preface

What is your purpose, and why would you want to know? Although many people ask questions about their life's purpose, it is extraordinary how few people actually know what it is. Many people even feel that this is a question that cannot be answered, a rhetorical or philosophical question. Nothing could be further from the truth. For each of us, there is indeed a specific answer to the question "Why am I here?"

Fully answering this question can fundamentally change your experience of life. People who know their purpose know where they're going, what they're doing, and, more importantly, they know why they're doing it. This shifts the basic emphasis of life from one of meeting needs, dealing with fears, and seeking happiness to following a path that leads to the greatest possible fulfillment, success, and meaning in life. Knowing your purpose satisfies a deep need that lives in everyone: the need for meaning, to have a positive impact, to have your presence and life felt by others. As people age, the yearning to leave some kind of legacy grows stronger. There is no greater legacy you can leave than living your life purpose to the fullest extent possible. This book is an attempt to create this experience for you, to make it possible for you to live a life of fulfillment, meaning, and success, in every possible sense of the word.

Why Another Book about Life's Purpose?

A quick look at Amazon.com or in the self-help section of any bookstore will tell you that plenty has been written about life's purpose.

Many of these books are fine, inspirational works, a credit to the topic and to their authors.

But much of what has been written is long on inspiration and short on methodology. It is a wonderful thing to hear about other people's purposes and how their lives have been changed by this knowledge. However, I assume that most people are interested in this subject because they want to know their own purpose, and they want the clarity, the feeling of connection to something larger, and the deep and persistent sense of fulfillment that knowing your purpose brings.

Most of the books that have been written about purpose articulate only one method for finding it, and sometimes none. Many devote a page or two to suggestions for finding your purpose. I find this sad, because there are specific, practical methods for finding your purpose that anyone can use. I have worked with hundreds of people to find their purpose, in both one-on-one and group settings. I have successfully used most of the methods in this book, on myself and on others. I can personally attest that it is a wonderful thing to know my purpose, and I reference it constantly when making decisions and facing tough situations.

Ultimately, this is a book about transformation, not inspiration. You may be inspired by what I write, but that is not my primary intention. My purpose is to equip you with the tools to transform yourself and your life. I am extremely interested in methods and techniques. I am keenly aware that no one is ever transformed solely through the act of reading. You will not be transformed by anything I write; you may be provoked, educated, and motivated. But in the end you will be transformed by what *you do* when you read this book.

But the real reason for writing this book is quite simply that I am compelled to do so. At the moment, I am sitting in front of my computer at 3AM, having been woken up by my son, who is sick tonight. As I lay awake in bed, this book started to write itself in my head for the hundredth time. I have been directed very specifically by my soul to write this book, and I would be a poor role model for my clients if I didn't take these instructions seriously.

Therein lies the downside of knowing your purpose. Now you might have to do something about it! Consider this a warning before you proceed any further in this book. Knowing your purpose can ask things of you, things that may be scary or uncomfortable. The path I lay out in this book is not for the dabbler, nor for the faint of heart. Living a purposeful life is a responsibility.

That said, I would not trade knowing and living my purpose for anything, with the possible exception of the health of my family. The clarity, the feeling of fulfillment, and the sense of direction I get from knowing my purpose is the most precious gift I can imagine. My sincerest hope in writing this book is that I can pass that gift on to you.

How to Use This Book

I have written this book with the assumption that you want to know your life's purpose. It is designed as a series of lessons and exercises whose intent is to reveal your purpose. The book will work best if you read it straight through, as written. If you encounter concepts and ideas that are familiar to you, you can skim those chapters, of course. But it is important that you have grounding in the concepts and ideas before attempting the exercises.

I strongly recommend that you do every exercise until you have completed Purpose Hunting, the set of exercises in the Indirect Access Methods chapter. After that, you will need to successfully and thoroughly complete at least one of the exercises in Chapter 4: Clearing a Path through the Ego. Then read the descriptions of the exercises in the Direct Access Methods chapters. You do not need to do all of the exercises or try all of the direct access methods. You only need one of these methods to work in order to find your purpose!

After you have read the descriptions of the self-study direct access methods, choose the method that seems most appropriate for you.

There are specific guidelines with each method, explaining the kind of person for whom the method works best. Try this method, following the instructions carefully. If it doesn't work, try another. Try all of the self-study methods that are appropriate for you until one of them works. (If one of the self-study methods is too confronting for you, or runs counter to a belief system that is important to you, by all means skip it.) There is no harm in trying a self-study method even if the recommendation says that it isn't suited for you. This just means that the chances of it working are smaller.

If you have tried all of the self-study methods and none of them has worked, you now have a choice. You can either go back and work more with ego blocks or you can hire a professional to help you with one of the facilitated methods. Properly trained professionals can help you clear ego blocks and find your purpose, but they usually cost money. Chapter 4: Clearing a Path through the Ego contains instructions on doing deeper self-study work with ego blocks. If you don't want to hire a professional, do this deeper work with ego blocks and then go back and try the self-study methods again.

If you choose to hire a professional, read about the facilitated methods. Choose the method that seems right to you, then seek a suitably qualified professional. Be sure to ask about the qualifications and certifications of the person you hire! Check both their credentials to use the technique that they employ as well as their experience finding clients' life purpose. Just because they hold a certification in neuro-linguistic programming or hypnotherapy, for example, doesn't mean they know anything about life purpose work.

A number of the exercises in this book will work much better if you do them with someone else. In particular, interpreting the results of any method or exercise is difficult to do by yourself. As you will see in the first chapter, your mind can play tricks on you and lead you away from your purpose. If you don't have a coach or other professional trained in life purpose methods, you and a friend can go through the book together.

Religion and Purpose

I have taken pains while writing this book to address the widest possible audience. I believe that the desire to know our purpose in life is a call that transcends religious and spiritual boundaries. I do not address my own religious beliefs in this book, for the simple reason that I consider them irrelevant to your exploration. Knowing my beliefs will not help you in the slightest in your quest. Your religious and spiritual beliefs, however, are highly relevant. In fact, they are a key to how you approach this process.

In many ways, the deeply religious have an advantage in the search for purpose. There is less suspension of disbelief required for some of the methods, for example. Also, some religious practices can develop you in ways that make finding your purpose significantly easier. If you are deeply religious, you will find that I do not mention God much or use other religious language. This is so that those readers who do not share your religious convictions may come along on this journey as well.

I encourage you to bring your beliefs with you; they will help you greatly in this endeavor. You may also find that some of the methods I articulate are inconsistent with your religion or your personal beliefs. No problem; skip them and use the others. One of the great advantages of providing multiple methods is that you can pick and choose from among the ones that are right for you. If your beliefs dictate that I must speak to you only in the terms of your religion, this book is not for you. In my attempt to reach as many people as possible, I may have included something that is not consistent with your religious system. But make no mistake about it: for the devout seeker, your faith is your strongest ally in this journey.

If you are not strongly religious, or perhaps even agnostic or atheist, it will not exclude you from this journey at all. I will not ask you to change your beliefs or take my word for anything. All that is required for you to come along is this: You must be willing to suspend some of your disbelief for the sake of exploration. You must accept, if only for the sake of argument, three things: 1) that your purpose already influences the course of your life, whether or not you are aware of it; 2) that some part of you already knows your purpose; and 3) that it is possible to communicate with the part of you that knows your purpose. That is all I ask. If you cannot accept that these three statements could possibly be true, perhaps this book will make a nice gift for a friend or loved one. If you are willing to try these on, then test them by pursuing the methods I am laying out here and draw your own conclusions.

A note to the very scientific. Congratulations if you've made it this far! Having been schooled at MIT, I am very familiar with what the skeptical mind can do with this material. First, a warning: I will offer no proof for my assertions. Any proof will come in the form of your experiences, not my information. The scientific method requires experimentation, does it not? Come along for the experiment.

> *"Everyone has been made for some particular work, and the desire for that work has been put into every heart."*
>
> – Rumi

Chapter One

What Does "Life Purpose" Mean?

Why Would I Want to Know My Purpose?

Our society sends us interesting messages, mostly through advertising and other electronic media. If what you see on TV and the Internet is to be believed, then there are many things you need to buy, and if you buy them, you will experience happiness, romance, and the envy of your peers. Most importantly, you need a lot of money to buy all of these expensive toys, drugs, vacations, cars, mansions, and electronic devices. The capitalist system is driven by the fuel of our desire for happiness and by the spending that results from this desire.

But there is an enormous, unexamined assumption underlying the pursuit of wealth and material goods, the assumption that these things will actually make you happy. Think back on the last time you got a raise, or received a big check in the mail. How did you feel? Pretty good, probably. But how long did that feeling last? An hour? A few days? A week, if you were really lucky?

And then the feeling was gone, and everything returned to normal. "Well," you may say, "it wasn't big enough. If I had won the lottery, then I would have stayed happy." That's what we're led to believe, anyway. Many states and countries need you to believe that; they use the proceeds from lottery tickets to balance their budget. But did you know that lottery winners have a higher rate of suicide than the rest of us? That within a few years they are usually worse off financially than they were before they won the lottery?

Of course, it's hard to obtain exact statistics. The organizations that run lotteries aren't exactly advertising the fact that the winners are usually worse off than before. But having worked with many miserable, high-level executives, I can verify that money won't make you happy (though lack of money can also create unhappiness!).

Okay, what about the things you buy with money: the vacations, the shopping, the expensive toys? Well, think back to when you bought that thing you really wanted: the car, the handbag, the big screen TV, the shoes. How did you feel? Pretty good, right? And how long did that feeling last? We're talking about fleeting gratification.

As you'll see later, the problem with these approaches is that they appeal very directly to a certain basic set of needs called "ego drives." The gratification of ego drives creates happiness that is notoriously short lived. It's like a narcotic drug. You need larger and larger doses to get your "fix," but the reality is that you're never fulfilled. This increasing need drives some people to extraordinary feats, working 80-hour weeks and putting up with unbelievable stress. Like any addiction, it's only a matter of time before the crash comes.

Sustained happiness cannot come from money, or from the things that money buys. Sustained happiness comes from meaning. It comes from growing, developing, and having a positive impact on the lives of others. This book will show you how you can grow, how you can develop, and how to make a contribution to the world that no one but you can make.

Life's Purpose

The search for meaning in life is as old as humanity. Great thinkers, prophets, philosophers, and teachers have addressed the question "What is the meaning of life?" For example, Rick Warren, author of the record-setting bestseller *The Purpose-Driven Life*, says that everyone's purpose is to worship God. Eckhart Tolle, in his book *A New Earth*, says that everyone's purpose is to bring the power of presence into the world. Many others have offered their answers to this question as well. I have no desire to offer you a single answer that addresses all of our purposes at once; I leave that to them. I am far more interested in the unique purpose that brought you into being and how your purpose is different from mine (or anyone else's). In short, I am not trying to find the meaning of *our* lives; I want to help you find the meaning of *your* life.

While I claim no expertise in the universal question of life's purpose, I am going to propose something that may seem even more radical: that you have an individual purpose, unique to you, and that you already know what it is. More accurately, I would say that some *part* of you already knows what it is. And if you are reading this book, chances are that you are not in very good communication with that part. The good news is that you can get in touch with this part of you and find your purpose; you are already on your way!

Now for the really good news. Finding your purpose can be simple and quick. When I first started working with people to find their purpose, I did what many coaches and consultants do: I gave them a free one-hour session to help them decide whether to hire me or not. I had to stop this practice within a month because too many potential clients were finding their purpose after the single free session and then never hiring me.

I don't mean to imply that it will be simple and quick for everyone. It took me about 20 years from when I began my exploration. And in retrospect, those 20 years were entirely necessary. It is my purpose to help you find your purpose. In order to learn to be a fit guide for others, I had to learn every technique, try every dead end, find my purpose, lose it, and find it again. I had to follow my path, abandon my path, and get back on it.

I call this period of searching in my life "wandering in the desert." I have spent a great deal of time wandering in this desert called "I want to know my purpose." It has gotten so that every dune and every oasis, every path and every dead end, are familiar to me. Knowing this desert so well, I am a very efficient guide. If you want to cross this desert, I can show you the way. In fact, I will show you many different ways. And if it turns out that you cannot or choose not to cross the desert, I can show you ways to live there comfortably.

Okay, let's get started. It's time to pack for our trip and check our maps. Before you try any of the methods I describe, it is important to have an understanding of where we are going and exactly what we are looking for. An understanding of the obstacles we may meet along the way will be useful as well. To this end, I want to define some terms and offer you a map. Since our destination is your purpose, and I am claiming that your purpose is already inside you, the only map that would be useful is a map of you. The rest of this chapter is devoted to a (somewhat simplified) depiction of the human psyche.

YOUR LIFE'S PURPOSE

Purpose answers the question "Why?" When I talk about life's purpose, I mean the "why" of your life. This "why" takes the form of questions like:

✓ Why are you here?
✓ Who are you meant to be?
✓ What are you meant to do?

Note that I am not asking, "What would you like to do?" The question of purpose is about what you are *designed* to do, what you're *meant* to do—not what you *like* or *dislike* doing.

This raises an interesting question. Is your purpose something that you get to choose, or is it something that has already been determined for you? Different people answer this question differently. If you believe that your purpose already exists, then your job is to discover what it is. The exercises in this book are designed to help you do just that.

If you believe that you get to choose a purpose, I have another question for you: Do you believe that any purpose you choose will be equally fulfilling for you? That is, do you believe that no matter what purpose you choose, you will be just as happy and successful? If you're like most people, then you believe that some purposes will serve you better than others. If that's the case, treat this book as an exploration to discover which possible purpose (or purposes) would suit you best.

If you believe that any purpose will serve you equally, don't waste your time reading this book. Choose a purpose and get going!

Now that we've explored what I mean by the word *purpose*, we need to begin an exploration of your inner landscape. The answers we seek are within you, so let's get to know the terrain.

The Ego

Every day each of us wakes up, makes decisions, accomplishes tasks, thinks, feels, eats, and so on. We experience desires, fears, and reactions. These things are normal, the regular fare of life. I am going to call the part of us that does these things, that has the thoughts and feelings, that makes the decisions, the "ego." "Ego" is Latin for "I," and that is exactly what I mean by it. When you say, "I like music," "I'm hungry," or "I want to know my purpose," the ego is the "I" that is speaking. Other terms for ego used in some traditions are the "persona," the "personality," the "conscious," or the "self" (with a small "s").

MAINTAINING YOUR IDENTITY

The ego has a very important function. It establishes and maintains our identity. As we go through life, we develop certain beliefs and opinions about ourselves. We create answers to the question "Who am I?" These answers come from things our parents and teachers said or did; our interactions with other people; feedback, insults, and compliments we receive; successes and failures; and observations of our own feelings, thoughts, and behaviors. In aggregate, all these experiences and input give us a sense of who we are, what we are "like." Imagine that someone asked you, "What kind of person are you?" You would respond with your ego's sense of your identity, the construct you have created to understand and identify yourself and your beliefs.

Interpreting information from the world around you is another very important function of the ego. We are constantly receiving far more information than our brain can process, and we need to filter this enormous flow of information and interpret it before we can make use of it. Because it is also responsible for maintaining your sense of identity, the ego filters and interprets the data it receives in a way that *reinforces* your sense of identity. More specifically, it tends to filter out any information that does not agree with your beliefs about yourself and the world around you.

All of the information you receive goes through a process of assigning meaning to things. Once most of the information has been filtered out, the ego has to decide what to do with the rest. For instance, a friend, spouse, or coworker does something, and you might naturally ask yourself, "Why did she do that?" In essence you are asking, "What does that action mean *to me*?" In particular, you want to know how she feels about you and how she is likely to behave around you in the future.

You can watch this happening in people around you. Have you ever had the experience of telling someone something and finding them completely unable to hear it? This is the ego's filtering function at work. People can become argumentative and even belligerent if you keep telling them something that doesn't agree with their beliefs. Some people will hear something different from what you said. Some will change the subject. Some will even leave the conversation rather than deal with anything that challenges their identity or belief systems.

You can also watch the assignment of meaning at work. One excellent example is when you leave a message for someone and don't get a call back. Just watch yourself interpret this input and assign meaning to it. The longer the delay, the more meaning you can create in this blank space. "He's angry at me," "he's busy," "something happened to him," and so on and so forth.

All of this filtering and interpreting goes on constantly, naturally, and invisibly. There is nothing wrong with it; I am describing a healthy ego at work. These ongoing processes allow you to function in the world. The sense of identity the ego creates sustains you. It gives you a frame of reference for making decisions, taking action, and interacting with others. When a vendor asks you whether you prefer chocolate or vanilla ice cream, you probably know how to answer. You can remember how you felt the last time you tasted each flavor, and you predict that you will probably feel the same way the next time you taste them. You assume that you will likely respond the same way today that you did yesterday. Without these memories and assumptions, you might have difficulty making any decisions at all.

KEEPING YOU SAFE

Besides all of this filtering and interpretation, the ego has two other very important functions. The first is safety. The ego is responsible for keeping you alive and healthy. It usually keeps you from walking in front of moving cars, insulting the boss and getting yourself fired, or doing things that will land you in jail. Safety can take subtler forms as well. The ego may prevent you from doing something that will lessen your friends' and coworkers' opinion of you, thereby protecting your image. It may

discourage you from revealing embarrassing details from your past on a
first date in order to decrease your chances of being rejected.

GETTING YOUR NEEDS MET

In addition to maintaining your identity and keeping you safe, the
ego is responsible for getting your needs met. We have a wide variety of
needs, as Abraham Maslow articulated so clearly in his seminal 1954
work, *Motivation and Personality*. The most basic are survival needs:
air, food, water, clothing, and shelter. You also have intimacy and social
relationship needs, like having a loving relationship or belonging to
groups of like-minded people. When your basic needs are met, the ego
turns its attention to things like fun, learning, expensive toys, and vacations. It may seek work that is fulfilling, rather than something that just
pays the bills.

Your ego is the part of you that experiences these needs, and it is the
part that takes action to meet them. As a result, the ego tends to see the
world through "need-colored" glasses. It wants to know what effect its
choices will make—how you are going to feel if you do this or do that.
"Will I like this new job if I take it? Will it pay enough? What will my
family think when I tell them about it?" These are the questions of an
ego attempting to determine what needs will be met (or not met) as the
result of a career decision.

To summarize, the ego has three principal responsibilities: 1) to
establish and preserve your identity, 2) to keep you safe, and 3) to meet
your various needs as best it can. In most people, the ego performs
these duties quite well, and they are able to function in society and
make the best of their circumstances.

This ego system does have several disadvantages, too. One is that
it resists growth and transformation. Since you filter and interpret
all information based on what you already believe to be true, it can
be challenging to change anything about yourself. Often, attempts at
new behavior feel "wrong," at least at first. This is why New Year's

resolutions are so notoriously short lived. A desire for improvement alone cannot stand up to the ego's pervasive and persistent process of self-reinforcement. It takes a pretty good plan and support system to overcome this natural resistance and make any significant changes. Most people lack the necessary understanding of how to achieve transformation in their life. Most people also lack support systems that will help them sustain any change they undertake.

Notice that I am *not* saying that the ego is a bad thing. A healthy, fully formed ego is a prerequisite for getting anything done and functioning in the world. The cry of "death to the ego" coming from many psychological and spiritual traditions does nothing but offer disrespect to the hardest working part of the psyche.

I'm going to leave this topic of the ego and its function here for now. We will return to it many times throughout the book. In particular, we will revisit this topic of self-reinforcing resistance to change after we find your purpose. It will be extremely important then, because you will be making decisions about how you want your life to change. In order for your desired changes to have a chance, you will need some means of getting past this tendency to stay in your current ego system.

The Unconscious

The description I just gave of the ego is quite all-encompassing. According to that definition, the ego contains every thought, feeling, belief, memory, desire, fantasy, and plan of which you are aware. It contains the sum total of who you believe yourself to be. So what else is there?

If the ego contains everything you know about yourself, then what remains is the things you don't know about yourself. All of the thoughts, feelings, and memories that don't match your belief system are edited by the ego and relegated to another part of your psyche that I will call the "unconscious." Other terms for this part of you include the "subconscious," the "shadow," and the "Self" (with a big "S").

It is difficult to talk about the unconscious. A properly functioning ego is masterful at turning your attention away from things that don't match your belief system. Everything in the unconscious is something that your ego already decided you aren't supposed to know. As one of my teachers used to say, "The problem with the unconscious is that it's unconscious."

It may help if I give some examples of how this works. There was a participant in a coach training I taught who discovered well into adulthood that she was molested as a child. If you had asked her in her 20s whether she was molested, she would have answered "no." She wouldn't have been deliberately lying; she truly didn't remember. When the event occurred, her ego decided that it was just too painful and upsetting to deal with. As a child, her identity simply wasn't strong enough to handle all the pain, grief, anger, shame, and other intense feelings that the event brought up. As an act of self-protection, her ego filtered the memory of the event and the feelings associated with it and buried them in her unconscious. This choice allowed her identity to continue intact, although somewhat bruised and damaged.

I have a friend who is rediscovering his anger. He is 55 years old. In his childhood environment, his grandfather was a consistently angry presence. Faced with this constant and upsetting input, his young ego decided that anger was a bad thing. It moved his own anger into his unconscious, where it lay buried for the next 50 years.

For both of these people, their identities are much stronger now than they were as children. They are no longer threatened by feelings that would have been overwhelming back then. Their egos have concluded that it is now safe to allow these feelings and memories to resurface, to move from the unconscious into their waking awareness.

The process of moving something from the ego into the unconscious is often called "disowning." We usually speak of a disowned child: the angry father slams the door and says, "I have no son." Disowning memories or feelings works the same way. The young boy says, "I am not angry." The young girl says, "I was not molested." Saying it doesn't make it so: the father still has a son; he is just unwilling to deal with him. The boy is still angry; he is just unwilling to acknowledge or feel his anger. The girl was still molested; she just doesn't remember it.

The fact that things are unconscious doesn't make them cease to exist. They still have an impact on our lives. Even though we are unaware of them, we can still sometimes see or feel their effects. Since we don't know the source, these effects can seem mysterious. The woman who forgot that she was molested as a girl remembered when she was in therapy. She was in therapy because she had crippling fears of intimacy whenever she was in a relationship with a man. Her sexual feelings were stimulating the hidden pain and shame that were associated with her first sexual experience. Although she didn't remember the molestation itself, she was still living with its consequences.

Some people interpret this conversation about the unconscious to mean that it contains dark, evil, or bad things. This is not necessarily the case. People often disown things that are wonderful and beautiful. Our identity can be just as easily threatened by our vastness, our brilliance, and our magnificence as by our anger, our need, and our pain.

We derive safety from denying the full scope of our gifts and abilities. A young girl displays a unique talent, a gift of intuition. She correctly senses something her parents are planning in secret, and she asks them if it is true. Her parents become uncomfortable. They are not sure what to do with her, or with her talent, and they feel inadequate and threatened. Sensing this, she chooses not to do it again. The talent goes into her unconscious. She behaves in ways that are acceptable to her parents and chooses to believe that she is not intuitive.

A teenage boy loves math and looks forward to class every day. He scores high on exams and homework. Some of his friends notice this and begin to ridicule him. They call him names. Like many teenagers, he is deeply concerned with fitting in. He begins to hang out with his friends more and to study less. He joins them in complaining about homework and the math teacher. His grades gradually decline. His gift for math has moved into his unconscious, and he has chosen to live from the belief that he is not good at math.

The things in our unconscious can be scary, and they can be beautiful and extraordinary. There is only one thing in common between the myriad things in our unconscious: that we do not know them.

The Soul

I contended at the very beginning that you already have a purpose and that part of you already knows what it is. I am going to call that part of you your "soul." This is a loaded term, and different religious and spiritual traditions define it many different ways. I do not intend to invoke religious definitions; for the purposes of this book I am simply defining "soul" to mean "the part of you that knows your purpose." I use this word because, of the thousands of words that most people use on a regular basis, it comes closest to what I mean. Of course, you are free to add whatever personal meaning you want to the term. Later, we will expand this term and encourage you to replace the word "soul" with language that is more specific and meaningful for you.

If you don't already know your purpose, then your purpose and your soul are both in your unconscious. Remember, the unconscious is by definition those things you don't know about yourself. There are many other things in your unconscious, but the part that interests us in this exploration is your soul, because it is the keeper of your purpose.

This is one of the points in the process where your religious and spiritual beliefs come into play. For example, if you are a monotheist (a Christian, Jew, Muslim, or Bahá'í, to name a few) then I would say that your soul is your interface to God. God put your soul in you to guide you and to remember your purpose, so that it wouldn't be lost when you forgot.

If you are an agnostic or atheist, or if your beliefs do not include a singular God, then what I just wrote is irrelevant for you. Your soul is simply part of your design. It is the part responsible for knowing your purpose, in the same way that your kidneys are responsible for filtering your blood and your ears are responsible for hearing. A belief in God is not required for most of the methods in this book to work.

The soul's responsibilities are very different from the ego's. The soul is not concerned with preserving your identity or your day-to-day safety and needs. It is charged with entirely different things.

1. The soul is the keeper of your purpose. It knows everything about who you are, including the things you have disowned and forgotten. It knows who you are meant to be and what you are meant to do. It makes decisions about how much of your purpose you are ready to know. I'll discuss this more later.

2. The soul is charged with your growth and development. Your soul isn't that concerned about how much money you are making at work and whether or not you like your job. It cares whether you are learning, growing, and transforming from the experience. Your soul may sometimes guide you towards unpleasant things so that you will develop or learn in specific ways. This is very confusing for the ego, which is usually trying to avoid pain and failure as best it can. Your soul is not trying to create just any growth and learning; it is trying to develop you in very specific ways that will serve your purpose. Your soul is going through its checklist of skills and experiences that you will need in order to fulfill your purpose. Its job is to make sure that the checklist is complete, that you have everything you need.

    Many of my clients retain me because they are at a crossroads in their career. They have been doing something successfully for a very long time, and now they suddenly find that they have lost their taste for it. This is confusing, since their ego has established their identity using their career: They know themselves as a lawyer, a doctor, or a salesman. They can't understand why they did this for so long and now it no longer fulfills them.

3. The soul is responsible for steering you along your path. There are many paths that lead to your purpose, and the soul is generally not attached to which one you take. Some people have a very open relationship with this process. For example, they pray and receive guidance. Many others are steered and guided in secret; they are unaware of their soul, and it influences them by affecting their circumstances and thereby influences their choices.

Many adults have had moments of connection with their soul. It can happen at any time: while staring at a beautiful vista during a hike, in church, during prayer or meditation, during sex, watching a child being born, or during intense moments of crisis.

I can remember at some critical junctions in my life hearing a quiet voice whispering in my ear, telling me which way to go. When I was a junior at MIT, I experienced a very strong need to know my purpose, but had no means to find it. My lack of purpose sapped my motivation to the point where I was no longer attending classes and failing most of my courses. I was in the Naval Reserve Officers Training Corps at the time, and the Navy fully expected me to suck it up and finish my degree. When I finally dropped out and took a job at RepliGen, a genetic engineering firm, the Navy decided to call me to active duty and send me off to boot camp. (This was well within their rights under the contract I had signed, and I knew it.)

I was doing very well at RepliGen, programming their scientific computers and setting up a Local Area Network (LAN) for the office staff. They offered to split the cost with me to hire a lawyer and get me out of my military obligation.

This was a very stressful and confusing time for me. I enjoyed my job, and the prospect of boot camp was not appealing. On the other hand, I had read the NROTC contract (a process that took nearly an hour) before I signed it, and I had been fully aware of what I was getting into. I had given the Navy the right to do what it was doing, and hiring a lawyer to break the contract seemed like a cheesy way out, whether I agreed with the Navy's decision or not.

It was then that I began to hear the voice of my soul for the first time. When I was at my most confused and depressed, I would sometimes hear a quiet voice say, "Go to boot camp." I wasn't sure where the voice was coming from, but I trusted it implicitly. It was frustrating because I couldn't get any more information, but it was also reassuring.

I took the voice's advice and went to boot camp. Swabbing decks and washing dishes for 150 sailors turned out to be just the tonic I needed. I learned nothing about my life's purpose, but the experience taught me the value of making an effort, purpose or no purpose. Going to MIT was certainly a more pleasant way to experience my seemingly meaningless life.

In the Navy, I also learned a tremendous amount about leadership. Every time I was promoted I was sent to two weeks of leadership training. This was many times the amount of training I received later as a director at Oracle Corporation. As I write this, I am planning my retirement after a very successful 23-year career in the Naval Reserve.

This quiet voice is represented in a very explicit way in the film *Field of Dreams*. In the movie, Kevin Costner's character is coached at different points to make choices that seem outrageous to his family and neighbors (and to his ego). In the end, of course, it all makes sense.

These experiences are often touching and memorable. People can feel the presence of something larger, something more patient and vaster than their ego. It can be very reassuring to know that your soul exists. If you haven't had such an experience, don't worry; it's not a prerequisite for this exploration.

> "No problem can be solved from the same level of consciousness that created it. We must learn to see the world anew."
>
> – Albert Einstein

Chapter Two

What Does Purpose Look Like?

The Components of Purpose

Our purpose itself is at the root of our being, the essence of who we are. It is fundamental, foundational. And it is as much about *being* as it is about doing. This makes it difficult to comprehend and describe, because our ego perceives our life and the world through doing. Many modern languages describe "doing" with far greater precision than they describe "being."

As best I can tell, each of us has a single purpose and it does not change in the course of a lifetime. However, our understanding of it changes as we age and explore, so our perception of our purpose will surely change.

Egos have some difficulty understanding purpose, because egos and souls do not speak the same "language." Egos tend to divide things into groups, to categorize and judge them. Souls do not. But ultimately this search for purpose is a search of the ego, because your soul already knows your purpose and does not need to search. So your purpose must be understood by your ego in order for your need to know to be satisfied.

In order to aid your ego in understanding your purpose, I have divided the single concept of "purpose" into three categories. These categories are arbitrary, a construction of my ego to assist yours. This is how our egos make sense of the world, by making categories. Without these categories, it is difficult for the ego to grasp the answers that the soul provides.

Essence

Essence is the most fundamental aspect of purpose, and the most difficult to describe. It is the aspect of purpose that is pure being, without doing. You *are* your purpose, even when you are standing still or asleep. This component of purpose is usually the most unconscious, that is, the least apparent to you.

This most basic state of our being has an impact, however. It is subtle and pervasive. Everyone you meet is affected by it, whether they are aware of it or not. And it forms the basis for the other two aspects of purpose. Imagine that each of us, everyone alive, is walking around in a vast field and it is dark. But it is not completely dark. Each of us is giving off a glow, shining our light on those nearby. There are subtle differences between the lights. Each is a slightly different color. No two are exactly alike. This subtle light is our essence. The part I am curious about is the unique quality of each person's essence, the "color" in this metaphor.

This metaphor also explains why it is so difficult for you to know and see your own essence, and how easy it is for others to discern it. Imagine that you were born with a bright red lightbulb on top of your head, shining all the time. Picture yourself walking into a roomful of people: one of the comments is "Wow, it sure just got red in here." And you say… "What's red?" Since everything you have ever seen has been under a bright red light, you don't even know what red looks like. You have no contrast by which to understand and describe "red." But other people do, because they can see the difference between when you are present and when you are not.

Essence operates just this way. When you arrive, so does your essence, and everyone around you is immediately affected by it, whether they are aware of it or not. But you are the person least likely to be able to identify it. It has been with you since the moment you were born, and you don't know what it's like *not* to be surrounded by it. Later we will discuss a method for using the perception of others to identify your essence.

What is essence like in practice? People often use feeling words to describe their essence, since most languages are not very good at describing being states. It can be a struggle to formulate essence in words. I have heard souls use words like "love," "joy," and "enlightenment" when describing a person's essence. Later you will see what purpose statements based on essence look like.

Knowing your essence can help your search for purpose in several ways. Whatever effect your essence is having on those around you, it would serve you (and potentially them) to know it. You can place yourself in situations where the effect you have is most needed. And whatever this most basic quality of being is for you, you can make your life more fulfilling by choosing activities (doing) that are more consistent with your essence (being).

Blessing

Blessing is the bridge between being and doing. It is when your essence moves into action. Think of it like this: You are a catalyst, a facilitator of some process. You do this process with those around you, probably unconsciously. Certain people need your process, and they are naturally drawn to you and you to them.

This process is pervasive. You have done it in some form in every job you've ever held and in every significant relationship you've ever had. You have been doing it since you were very young. When you are most successful and most fulfilled, you are doing your blessing.

Let me use an example. I know a skilled coach whose blessing is to heal men who didn't get enough love from their mothers. Before working with me, she didn't know that this was her blessing. She was just going about her business, working with men and women. But she had noticed that certain kinds of men were drawn to her, attracted to her. They usually experienced this attraction as romantic, but the relationships that resulted were disastrous.

When she came to understand her blessing, she could see why this had been occurring. It enabled her to channel these men into more appropriate coaching relationships, where they could get the help they needed.

It is useful to break the blessing down into the actual steps. Here is my fellow coach's blessing, step-by-step:

1. A man is wounded, having not received enough love from his mother.

2. He is drawn to the coach, and she to him.

3. He begins to open up. He tells her all about himself, things he has never told anyone, because he trusts her right away.

4. She tells him exactly how she sees him, what she sees in his soul. She has the ability to see past the surface, the mask, to his inner child. She tells him who he truly is.

5. This builds his belief in himself, his love for himself. It makes him stronger.

6. At some point, he becomes self-sufficient and the relationship ends.

It is important to remember that the blessing is usually unconscious. You are doing it all the time without realizing it. As I said earlier, this woman had a series of relationships where this pattern played out, until she was able to understand that this was part of her purpose.

To derive the maximum benefit from knowing your purpose, you need to be fully aware of your blessing. You must understand completely the different aspects and nuances of it. Many people have a simple, vague purpose statement, something like, "to teach" or "to help people achieve their dreams." This is not nearly specific enough to qualify as a fully expressed blessing. Teach whom? What are the specific steps of finding someone's dreams? There are many more details to understand about a blessing, and the details matter.

Your blessing is the key to finding the right job or career. Purpose does not specify a career, but your blessing will help you understand which careers are the best choices for you. For example, a woman with a blessing for motivating downtrodden people will likely feel unfulfilled as a corporate audit accountant but fulfilled as a neighborhood activist, a city councilperson, a social worker, or writing a column in the local paper. The more closely your job responsibilities match your blessing, the more fulfilled and successful you will be.

Mission

A mission is just what it sounds like: a specific task that needs to be performed. When I think of mission, I remember the classic TV show *Mission: Impossible* (and the more recent Tom Cruise movies). "Good morning, Mr. Phelps. Your mission, should you choose to accept it, is to…" Just as in the TV show, your mission is an instruction that is given to you. And just like in the TV show, you can accept it or decline it.

A mission can take many forms. It can be an instruction to serve a specific group of people, a problem you have been designed to solve, or a change that you are to create in the world. As we'll see later, in the course of finding your purpose you may be given many instructions. Your mission is the highest level instruction you've been given by your soul.

Your mission is invariably a specific application of your blessing and essence. While there may be many ways you could do your blessing, your mission emphasizes a particular way or a particular outcome.

It may ask you to use your blessing with a particular group or to have some specific impact.

For example, my blessing is to "show people their path." In practice, this usually means helping people identify and live their purpose. There are many situations that call for this service, usually when people are at a crossroads in their lives. Here are some examples of circumstances that cry out for path-showing:

- ✓ Mothers whose children have recently left home
- ✓ People who have recently been fired or laid off
- ✓ People being released from prison
- ✓ Newly retired people
- ✓ People who have been diagnosed with a life-threatening disease

All of these are situations that would benefit greatly from finding life's purpose, and all are well within the scope of my blessing. However, I've been instructed to help *leaders* find their path. When I am true to my mission, I restrict myself to high-level leaders and large organizations that are meant to change the world.

Some of the better known people of our time were driven by their mission: Mother Teresa, Dr. Martin Luther King, Jr., and Mahatma Gandhi. Their choice to pursue their respective mission affected hundreds of millions of lives. In each case, the task was specific and formed the basis of their life's work.

Not all missions are so public or so sweeping in scope. One of my wife's dance students is a forensics expert; she specializes in identifying remains found in mass graves. Her name may never appear on the front page of a newspaper, but many of the tragedies in Bosnia and Africa have begun to heal with her help.

For many people the mission is the scariest aspect of purpose, and usually the last to be revealed. Most people have mixed feelings about having a mission: They both desire to have the meaning and guidance a mission provides and fear the responsibility such a task demands.

For this reason, the soul is often reluctant to disclose the details of the mission. If the mission is disclosed prematurely, the ego could, out of fear, shut down progress towards the purpose. "Who am I to pursue such a mission?" "What will people think of me?" I have felt this feeling of "clenching" in response to my mission, and so have many of my clients. These concerns are healthy and normal, and a person usually must deal with them before the mission can be revealed.

I have experienced changes in my mission over time. For years, the highest level instruction I had been given was to help leaders and organizations find their purpose. I came to understand, however, that this wasn't really the mission. This was a strategy for changing how business operates, while the true mission is to change how capitalism functions. My task is to change business from something that is driven by ego needs and desires to something that is driven by purpose.

Now, having lived and spoken that mission for several years, I am beginning to see that even that is just a strategy for a larger mission. The larger mission is to change society and how it operates, and altering the business paradigm is a means of achieving that goal. Over the next few years I expect this larger mission to come into sharper focus.

This brings up an interesting point. Your mission can change at any time! Your soul can give you a new instruction that is at a higher level than your current mission. (That's what keeps happening to me.) As I said earlier, your soul will tend to withhold the really global, sweeping stuff (if any) until you're ready to hear it.

> *"Every individual has a place to fill in the world, and is important, in some respect, whether he chooses to be so or not."*
>
> – Nathaniel Hawthorne

Chapter Three

Indirect Access to Purpose

There are two types of methods for finding your purpose: indirect access and direct access. In indirect access methods, we use the available evidence to construct a picture of your life's purpose. This is kind of like the work of a crime scene investigator, using clues to piece together what occurred. In a crime scene investigation, it is often difficult to tell exactly what happened, though it is usually possible to get a rough idea. The same is also true using indirect access methods. It may be difficult to construct an exact sense of purpose using them, but it is usually possible to get a rough idea.

Direct access methods entail communicating directly with your soul and asking it what your purpose is. This results in a much clearer picture of your life's purpose than that achieved by indirect access methods. I discuss this in Chapter 5: Direct Access to Purpose. Despite the much greater clarity provided by direct access methods, indirect access is by far the most common way of seeking purpose. This is because indirect access methods work for nearly everyone, while some direct access methods work for as few as 10% of the people who attempt them. When books on life purpose provide any means for finding your purpose, it is almost always an indirect method. Similarly, coaching schools usually train their students in indirect methods, if they provide any life purpose training at all.

There is a rich history of indirect access methods, particularly in the career counseling field. For example, the bestselling book *What Color Is Your Parachute?* includes an indirect access method that hints about your life's purpose as part of a career search. Jim White's book *What's My Purpose?* uses a series of indirect access methods to get a ballpark purpose based on skills. Many people calling themselves "life purpose coaches" each have their own list of favorite questions they use to employ an indirect access method for finding their client's purpose. While the questions vary, the basic method remains the same. All of the methods of this nature I am equating with Method 1: Purpose Hunting, which you will read about shortly. This is because regardless of the nature of the questions, the process is the same. The person seeking their purpose is asked a series of questions, and the answers are used to draw conclusions about their purpose.

In this book, I have included two indirect access methods and nine direct access methods. (There is also an additional method towards the end. You can use this method to live a purposeful life even if none of the others work for you.) I strongly recommend that you do the indirect access methods before attempting any of the others. There are two reasons for this. First, almost everyone can learn something about their purpose using these methods. Second, they are great warm-up exercises. Doing the indirect access methods first will make it easier for the direct access methods to work.

How Indirect Access Works

Indirect access methods are called "indirect" because they involve the ego speculating, deducing, and inferring the contents of your purpose without any direct knowledge of it. This means that you use clues and evidence available at the surface levels of your psyche to determine what your purpose might be. There is a tremendous advantage to this way of piecing together your purpose: It works for almost anyone. This is why indirect access methods are so popular.

However, there is a tremendous disadvantage as well. Indirect access methods are far less accurate than direct access methods. The reason is that your ego, not your soul, makes decisions about what your purpose is. Not only is your ego not well informed about your purpose, it is also not an objective observer. Your ego has a tremendous stake in the outcome of the process, because your purpose will influence your life in profound ways. Therefore, your ego has lots of incentive to tamper with the process and edit and censor your purpose while you're using an indirect access method. For this reason, it is critical to get other people involved when you are using indirect access methods. Using indirect methods by yourself is far less accurate than when you use them with other people.

Method 1: Purpose Hunting™

Remember that the soul's main function is to guide the development of the ego. The soul does this by influencing your decisions and helping you to choose things that will develop you in ways that serve your purpose. This often happens unconsciously, without you even being aware of it.

The soul also "arranges" experiences for you that will cause you to grow and develop. These experiences can sometimes be unpleasant, such as car accidents, being fired or laid off, and losing loved ones. But often it is our worst experiences that teach us the most. Don't worry for the moment about how the soul "causes" these things to happen; suffice to say that it doesn't operate in the same linear, cause-and-effect world in which most people live. What is important to understand is that your soul often steers you towards learning opportunities that your ego would naturally avoid.

Along the way, as you try out different things (jobs, relationships, activities), you act in ways that are in alignment with your fundamental purpose, and also in ways that are not. While you may be unaware of your purpose, these two ways of behaving usually feel very different when you reflect on your actions and the results they produced.

If you are like most people, when you are out of alignment with your purpose, you find obstacles at every turn. You have to muster up energy and will to complete things. You are not satisfied by your accomplishments, or the satisfaction is fleeting. You wonder why you're doing what you're doing and imagine greener pastures. Life is dry, empty, and full of drudgery. I call this experience "slogging." Here is how Joe, a participant in the Know Your Purpose Workshop, described his experience of slogging, before he discovered his purpose:

> "In all areas of my life, I was experiencing difficulties and confusion, feeling anxious and dragged down. I tried many different jobs and was frustrated. Anything I tried had me in turmoil; my inner voice was complaining that it wasn't good enough. I questioned what I was doing there. I feared I would never feel the satisfaction of success. I was unable to express my purpose. Any words I put together always felt like something was missing, that although it might make some sense, it wasn't complete, it wasn't right. I felt knots in the pit of my stomach and an empty, hollow feeling in my heart. I had the continual angst that I'd never get it right, that I'd never know my purpose. I kept looking but couldn't find the answer. I had a deep, sad sense that I had lost my way and that life had little meaning for me anymore. I could see nothing right or good about what anyone else was doing, and I saw that my relationships were suffering."

When you are doing things that are in alignment with your purpose, it feels very different. Your soul gives you positive feedback. This usually means you feel fulfilled, passionate that you are making a difference. Things happen easily. Chance coincidences seem to support your goals and projects. This is called "serendipity" or "synchronicity." Your efforts produce results, seemingly with little effort. Many people refer to this state as one of "flow." After Joe took the Know Your Purpose Workshop and found his purpose, here is how he described his experience:

> "At the workshop, I quickly began to receive some information about my purpose. It was a relief to have this first glimpse, and it gave me hope. I began to feel alive and open. It required self-examination to really clear the way. Then with little fanfare, old stuff just fell away, and there it was. My purpose was simple and clear, and nothing like what I had imagined previously. I felt that I had finally come to know who I truly am.
>
> "I am living in a different place now than I have been for 40 years! It's a different universe now; life is so much richer! I am lighter, happier, and having fun! I have let go of so many behaviors that used to run me, and I've become a better husband and father as a result. Job opportunities are being offered to me without my even having to look for them, and other good things are just showing up. As my sense of my place in the world has become clearer, my choices have been clearer and easier, and the opportunities more accessible. Knowing that I am living on purpose has helped me to relax and enjoy who I am. I had no idea how joyful it could feel just to be me."

It is important to note that your soul is not attached to you making purposeful choices and being on purpose. You will learn and grow either way, and your soul is primarily interested in your growth and learning. Whether you enjoy that experience is of great interest to the ego, but not to the soul.

This method makes use of the experiences of being in alignment to gather information about your purpose. By looking back over your life, you can see the times when you were on purpose. By looking for similarities in those times or events, we can draw conclusions about your purpose. I call this process "Purpose Hunting."

Here's how it works. As I said earlier, you can make use of the differences in your experiences, using your reactions to determine when you are in alignment and out of alignment with your purpose. Looking back over your life, it's possible to identify times when you were in the flow and then to identify commonalities in these experiences. These commonalities can give you important information about your purpose.

In this method, we will only make use of the times when you were on purpose. Drawing commonalities between the times when you were off purpose will tell us what your purpose *isn't*, but this information is much less useful than knowing what your purpose *is*.

The questions that follow are divided into two different journaling exercises. The first exercise looks for the places in your life when you have experienced flow. The second exercise seeks to get additional information from other kinds of questions. Do both journaling exercises before trying to interpret your answers and drawing any conclusions about your purpose.

Exercise: Journaling "Flow" Experiences

Choose two or three of the following questions that are easiest for you to answer. For example, I'm not a particularly passionate guy, so when I think about when I've felt most "passionate," not a lot comes to mind. On the other hand, when I think about when my life has had meaning, I immediately can think of jobs and periods of time when I had that experience. (A friend of mine says that he falls in love four times on the way to his seat on an airplane. The "passion" question probably isn't the best one for him, either.) Give specific examples of events or periods of time, not generic patterns ("In the winter of 1984 when I went skiing on Whistler," not "when I'm skiing"). They can be work-related or not.

It's also best not to use events like the birth of your child, your wedding, or being in a beautiful natural setting as answers to the questions. Although these may well be expressions of your soul, they tend to be universally moving experiences and won't give you much information about your unique and distinct purpose.

Again, use whichever questions work for you. You need a total of 3-5 examples (from all of the questions in this exercise, not 3-5 for each question). Okay, now for the questions.

1. When are the times in your life when you've felt most passionate?

2. When are the times in your life when you've felt most fulfilled?

3. When are the times when you've felt your life has had the most meaning?

4. When are the times when you've felt most aligned?

5. When are the times when you've experienced ease, flow, synchronicity, and serendipity?

Exercise: Journaling Additional Purpose Information

Also answer all of these questions that you can. They will provide additional information that can be used to discover features of your purpose.

1. What did you always want to be or do when you grew up?

2. What are you uniquely designed and prepared to do?

3. List the things to which you're consistently drawn. What about them draws you?

4. If you had a year to live, what would you spend your time doing?

5. You have lived to a ripe old age and you are lying on your death-bed. You look back with satisfaction over a long, fulfilling life. You feel satisfied and fulfilled because you did or were what?

6. You have won the lottery and all of your financial needs are handled. You spend a year traveling, buying expensive toys, and having fun, and then get bored and decide it's time to do something meaningful with your newfound freedom and resources. What do you do?

7. Imagine that all the issues and wounds from your childhood were chosen deliberately by your own soul in order to develop and hone you. How have your psychological issues trained and developed you? What skills or gifts have you received or learned from them?

Only answer the last question if you have done a significant amount of work on your own psychology, through therapy, workshops, or some venue that directly addressed your childhood emotional wounds and your psychological development. The question will probably not produce much of value if you haven't explored your early formative experiences in this way.

How to Evaluate Your Journaling

The most important thing you can do is to get help evaluating your journaling. It is extremely difficult for you to see your own patterns objectively. If you do this alone, there is an excellent chance that you will not learn anything new or interesting about yourself. The person or people who help you should be supportive and interested in the topic; don't ask your friend who thinks all of this stuff is nonsense. If you have the money, there are life purpose coaches you can hire who are skilled at evaluating this kind of information. If not, see if you can interest some friends or a partner in doing this exercise with you. Everyone can do the journaling on their own, then get together and take turns sharing the results. (This is what we do in my teleseminars and workshops.)

The task in going over your answers is to find patterns. It doesn't matter which question you were answering; just take all of the answers together and sift through them, looking for the commonalities and patterns. These patterns are sometimes literal and sometimes more symbolic or generic. You need to use a little imagination and creativity in order to see the more symbolic ones. You can find the patterns in a number of different ways:

✓ Patterns in behavior – you keep finding examples of the same kinds of activities in your answers. This is the simplest type of pattern and the easiest to find. The activities that keep recurring are likely related to the blessing aspect of your purpose.

✓ Patterns of feeling – the behaviors and incidents vary, but in each case you have a consistent feeling. This feeling state is probably related to your purpose in some way.

✓ Patterns of being – the behaviors and incidents vary, but in each case you are being the same way, or being the same kind of person. This being state is probably related to the essence aspect of your purpose.

✓ Symbolic patterns – while the activities and incidents are different, they are all symbolically representative of the same thing. This symbolic pattern is probably an expression of your purpose.

The symbolic patterns are the most difficult to see and also the most powerful. It is highly unlikely that you will find them without the help of a coach or a group of fellow purpose hunters.

Here are a couple of case studies to show you how to connect the answers to produce a pattern. I will use myself in the first example. Here are the activities in my life that have given me the most fulfillment and meaning:

- ✓ Coaching people and companies to find their higher purpose
- ✓ Navigating ships for the Navy
- ✓ Counseling subordinates at Oracle Corporation on their career paths
- ✓ Helping companies to define their mission, vision, and values

Can you see the common thread between these things? As activities, they bear little resemblance to one another. My being state isn't even particularly consistent between them: When I'm on the bridge of the ship using a sextant, I am a very different person than when I am talking to people's souls about their purpose. The common thread here is a symbolic one: They are all ways of showing people their path. And that is my blessing: showing people their path.

This illustrates the difference between soul and ego values once again. While my ego definitely prefers being a highly paid management consultant to being an enlisted man in the Navy, my soul has no such preference and barely distinguishes between them. My soul is primarily concerned with the fact that I am fulfilling my purpose, not with how much I am being paid for doing it.

Having realized that this is my blessing, I can see times throughout my life when I have done this. When I was in college, I was frequently attracted to women who were a little "lost." Once I helped them find their way, the relationship usually ended (having served its unconscious purpose). Here are some other ways I have expressed this blessing:

- ✓ Orienteering (a sport that involves running through the woods with a map and compass)
- ✓ Giving driving or walking directions to people who are lost
- ✓ Creating large-scale computer software implementations that enable companies to plan their financial future

I will use my college roommate as the second example of a symbolic link between purposeful activities. He is very passionate about his favorite hobby, photographing nudes. He works extensively with light and shadow effects, spending hours getting things just right. He did some beautiful photos of my wedding, working in his darkroom and developing them himself.

He also has been very fulfilled working for many years as an electrical engineer. His specialty is designing integrated circuit chips that interpret the sound echoes produced by sonograms and render them into visible images. Of course, sonograms are devices typically used to create images of the interior of the human body. You have probably seen sonograms of a baby still in its mother's uterus.

To our outer mind these two activities are almost completely unrelated, but both are direct expressions of his purpose: "to illuminate the human form." Both his amateur photography and the computer chips he creates show us images of the human body that we would not ordinarily see.

This example also illustrates an important feature about how purpose integrates with work. What do you imagine might happen if my buddy left his job making sonogram chips and started making machines that used similar technology to show images of what's below the surface of the earth, say, to detect earthquake fault lines or untapped oil reserves? Normally we might think that this would be a fine career choice and a natural expression of his skills. But it's not aligned with his purpose! He would become unfulfilled quickly, and the resulting drain on his motivation would make it difficult for him to succeed.

These two examples illustrate how a more subtle link between the answers can also be the most powerful one. They also demonstrate why you will have a much easier time identifying the patterns in your answers if you enlist the help of a coach or others who are in pursuit of their purpose! It is very difficult to see these kinds of subtle patterns yourself and much easier for others to see.

While you and those who are helping you are working with your answers, make a list of any patterns that you notice. At this point don't worry about which ones are "right" or "true," just keep writing them down. Keep going until everyone starts to run out of ideas.

Now it's your turn to sift through this list of patterns. Read through them, preferably out loud. Notice what you feel as you look at and say each pattern. The ones that elicit the strongest emotional or physical response *of any kind* are the ones you should pay attention to. Circle these patterns.

Common responses that people have to patterns are:

- ✓ Knowing it is true
- ✓ Hoping it is false
- ✓ A feeling of passion or elation
- ✓ A feeling of fear
- ✓ Embarrassment or shame
- ✓ A deep sense of alignment or "rightness"

Any of these reactions, or any other strong reaction, is usually a sign that the pattern that caused it is related to your purpose in some way. If you have no strong reactions, feel for mild ones. Don't question or judge the reaction you had; just circle the pattern on the list that caused it.

Now you have your short list of winners. This is the place to stop. At this point, many coaches would have you start constructing a purpose statement. I strongly recommend against this. Remember, this is the least accurate of all of the methods. Any purpose statement you create now risks being a construction of your ego. Write down your short list of purpose patterns and move on to another method. If none of the other methods work, then you can use this list to work out your purpose statement.

Before we go on, I want to note that there are many variations on this exercise. Many different books, coaches, and training programs have their sets of purpose questions; these aren't the only ones you can use. Also, there are different ways to test the accuracy of the answers; emotional reaction is only one.

Method 2: The Essence Conversation

Nearly all of the indirect access methods I have encountered are basically equivalent to Method 1: Purpose Hunting. However, I have encountered one ingenious indirect access method that does not share some of the serious disadvantages of Purpose Hunting and similar question-and-answer approaches. This method is the Essence Conversation, created by Hans Phillips of Accomplishment Coaching. While this method only yields information about the essence aspect of purpose, it does a far better job of it than typical indirect access methods. This is because it employs the perspectives of people other than you to deduce your essence. This is very appropriate, since, as I've explained, essence is invisible to the person who lives it—much like a fish in water cannot see the water because it is everywhere.

The method is very simple. You ask ten people in your life, "What happens when I come into the room? What shows up when I show up?" These questions speak directly to the invisible effect of essence, that is, the impact that your presence has on other people without you actually engaging in any activity whatsoever. Like any other indirect access method, you are the person least qualified to interpret the results. In order to get the best results from this method, you should employ the services of someone trained in it. So far as I know, only Accomplishment Coaching trains people to interpret the results from this method. You can find information about Accomplishment Coaching in the resources in the Appendix.

Chapter Four

Clearing a Path through the Ego

If you're like most people, indirect methods will not provide enough clarity to satisfy you. The main reason that indirect methods work for so many people is that they *don't* communicate directly with the soul. It is less of a risk to use those methods. As a result, they also provide vaguer, more approximate results. Direct communication with the soul raises the stakes in the search for purpose. Once the ego gets the idea that the soul is going to say what the purpose is, it usually gets nervous about it. Your ego's resistance to knowing your purpose is the number one obstacle in this exploration. When I work one-on-one with clients, I spend a month or more dealing with their fears and concerns first.

I say this to illustrate why it is so important to deal effectively with ego resistance. If you do not work with your ego's resistance, your chances of finding your purpose via the direct access methods are quite small. You may think you have no resistance to finding your purpose, but if that were true you would probably already know it!

What follows are several different methods for clearing the fears, doubts, and limiting beliefs that are keeping you from being clear about your purpose. **You must use at least one of these methods successfully, or none of the direct access methods will work.** Trying to overcome or ignore your fears will not work. Assuming that you don't have any fears will not work. Having worked with hundreds of clients, I have met a total of perhaps four people who could find their purpose directly without first clearing a path through the ego. These four individuals represent very well what it takes to create an ego that isn't managed by fear:

✓ A Christian woman who had surrendered her life to God fully. She had spoken to God daily in prayer for decades and didn't worry about what tomorrow would bring, trusting Him completely.

✓ A Buddhist man who had meditated daily for decades and held his entire life as a spiritual journey. His meditation practice was so important to him that he bought a separate house, which he devoted solely to his spiritual practices.

✓ A woman who was a trained professional channeler. Connecting to forces outside of her ego was her day job.

✓ A man who had done hundreds of medicine journeys, to the point that his psyche had been completely transformed by the experience. (See Method 11: Journey Work for a description of this practice.)

Note that I do not fall into any of these categories; dealing with my fear and resistance to finding my purpose was a lot of work. I continue to experience fear and resistance to manifesting my purpose, though things are much smoother now. For the 98% of us who have not eradicated all trace of fear and resistance from our ego, then, dealing constructively with it is a necessary step on the path to purpose.

Working with Fears

The first and simplest method of clearing a path to your purpose deals very directly with your fears. It is a quick method, usually requiring about an hour and a half to complete. (Some of the other methods can take weeks!) It can also be uncomfortable. Most people have some trepidation about learning their purpose. This is normal, because the search for purpose takes us into the unknown. If you don't know your purpose, you have no idea what its ramifications will be.

This is a lot like the scene in the movie *The Matrix* when Morpheus offers Neo two pills. Take the red pill, see the matrix. Take the blue pill, wake up in your bed and believe whatever you choose to believe. But if you take the red pill, there is no going back. If you find your purpose, it will change your life. You cannot put the genie back in the bottle.

The two exercises that follow can create the permission you will need to access your purpose directly, if you are thorough and follow the instructions carefully.

Exercise: Identifying Ego Blocks

This is a really simple exercise. Get a piece of paper and a pen, or open a document on your computer, and write down any fears or reservations you are having about finding and living your purpose. If you were to find it *right now*, why might that be a problem? If you lived your purpose from this moment forward, what could possibly go wrong? This is important. Don't pick up the book again until you have listed them all.

Exercise: Worst-Case Scenarios

Ready? Do you have your list of fears, concerns, and reservations? The parts of your psyche that are most concerned about finding your purpose usually employ "worst-case scenario" thinking. That is, they look at each risk in terms of the worst possible thing it could lead to.

This method uses those worst cases to deal directly and effectively with your fears and concerns.

To understand how this process works, let's take a common fear. Many people have the fear, "What if I can't make money doing my purpose?" This is a perfectly valid question. The problem isn't that you have the question; the problem is that you have never answered it. Well, what if you found your purpose, did it, and didn't make any money at it? What then? If you knew the answer, then you would have a plan. If you had a plan, you wouldn't need to worry. If you didn't need to worry, then getting really clear about your purpose wouldn't be a problem.

This exercise will deal very directly with each fear you identified in the previous exercise. You must do it with each and every fear, and you must follow the directions precisely.

1. You will need your list of fears from the previous exercise.

2. Start with the first fear from your list. Ask yourself, "What's the worst thing that could happen if this fear came true?" Write down the answer. Be specific, and make sure it's the worst thing you can imagine. Don't worry about whether it's realistic or not.

3. You now have a new, deeper fear. Reread your answer, and then ask the question again: "What's the worst thing that could happen if *that* happened?"

4. Keep repeating Step 3 until one of the following happens:

    a. You start to repeat yourself (i.e., the thing you come up with is essentially the same as the thing you came up with the last time you asked yourself the question).

    b. Your mind is completely blank because you are unable to think of anything worse. (Hint: For most people, dying is NOT the worst thing they can imagine happening to them. Don't stop there! If you died, what's the worst thing that could happen then? Or, what would be worse than dying?)

c.   You conclude that it's actually not a problem at all; you would be okay if this happened. (An example of this: A woman in a workshop once said, "My fear is that if I found and lived my purpose, my husband might leave me. What's the worst thing that could happen if he left me? Well, he's a total jerk; I guess it wouldn't really be a problem if he left.")

When one of these three things happens, you have "hit bottom." It's important that you go as deeply as possible in this phase of the exercise. It may start to seem silly or unrealistic; don't let this stop you. Don't try to solve problems and make things better; keep working with the worst possible thing that could happen.

If you concluded that it wasn't a problem at all, go back to Step 2 and pick a new fear from your list. Keep going!

5.   If you repeated yourself or couldn't think of anything worse, continue to work with this fear. Now ask yourself, "If I knew that this would happen if I tried to find and live my purpose, would I still want to?" It doesn't matter what the answer is; all that's important is that you have a clear "yes" or "no." "Maybe" is not helpful; try to get to a "yes" or a "no." Very important: If you answer "no," you can still find your purpose, so don't worry about it.

6.   If you answered "yes," you are complete with this fear. Go back to Step 2 and start working with another one.

7.   If you answered "no," ask yourself, "At what point would I stop pursuing my purpose if this fear started to come true?" Write down the answer in a new list titled "Constraints." For example, if your fear is that you wouldn't make enough money doing your purpose and might end up dying alone in an alley with AIDS,

the point at which you stop might be something like, "If I can't pay the mortgage on my house and feed my wife and kids, I'll stop doing my purpose and find some way to make money." In this case, you would add the following constraint to your list: "I must be able to pay the mortgage and feed my wife and kids." This constraint is a condition of pursuing your purpose. If the constraint isn't met, you won't live your purpose. You are now complete with this fear; go back to Step 2 and start working with another one.

8. Once you have repeated this process with ALL of the fears on your list, ask yourself whether you missed any fears. There might be one or two more; it's important to be thorough! Repeat the process with any additional fears you can think of.

9. Once you've processed all of the fears you can think of, read the list of constraints from Step 7.

10. Ask yourself, "If none of these things happens, do I choose to find and live my purpose?"

11. Once you answer "yes" or "no," you are complete.

If you answered "no" in the final step, you do not have permission from your ego, and using the direct methods probably will not work. This could happen for one of several reasons. One reason is that finding your purpose may not be that important to you. More likely is that your list of fears is incomplete, or your list of constraints is incomplete. This exercise only works if you have been completely thorough and have left no stone unturned. You must work with every fear, no matter how irrational it may seem. I've seen workshop participants process lists of 40 fears before finding their purpose!

If you answered "yes" in the final step, you now have permission from your ego. You will now likely be able to successfully use at least one of the direct access methods to find your purpose.

Some people notice a palpable shift in feeling at this point. You may feel a lightening, as if something has been lifted off of you. You may have experienced strong emotions while working with your fears. People have all kinds of feelings after doing this exercise, and some people have no feelings at all. Notice what you are feeling.

If you worked the process deeply, creating really awful worst-case scenarios, you probably noticed an interesting thing: For most people, nearly every surface fear ultimately leads to only one or two worst-case scenarios. It turns out that even though people think they have many fears, they really only have one or two. The rest are just different heads of the same beast, like the multi-headed hydra that Hercules slew as one of his labors.

Example

Here's how it might look if you worked a single fear all the way through this process. Let's assume you had the fear that you wouldn't be able to make enough money living your purpose. Here's how the process could progress:

Question: "What's the worst thing that could happen if I found my purpose and couldn't make money at it?"

Answer: "I wouldn't be able to pay my mortgage."

Question: "What's the worst thing that could happen if I couldn't pay my mortgage?"

Answer: "My family and I would be out on the street."

Question: "What's the worst thing that could happen if my family and I were out on the street?"

Answer: *"My wife and children would leave me."*

Question: *"What's the worst thing that could happen if my wife
             and children left me?"*

Answer: *"I would be alone for the rest of my life."*

Question: *"What's the worst thing that could happen if I were
             alone for the rest of my life?"*

Answer: *"I would be miserable and die alone."*

Question: *"What's the worst thing that could happen if I were
             miserable and died alone?"*

Answer: *"I would be abandoned in an alley and ignored until
             I died."*

At this stage the scenario has repeated itself, so this fear has reached "bottom." (Note that for people who believe in life after death, the process would continue to additional nightmare scenarios!) Now we look for the constraint(s), if any:

"If I knew that finding and living my purpose would lead to dying alone in an alley, would I do it anyway? No!"

"When would I stop?"

"If I couldn't pay my mortgage, I would stop pursuing my purpose and go earn the money."

In this scenario, the constraint would be "I must be able to pay my mortgage." This is a boundary and a commitment: "If I can't pay my mortgage, I will quit pursuing my purpose until this problem is handled." This agreement I make with myself makes it safe to learn and pursue my purpose. Now I would need to do this with each of the other fears I have, using the process above.

Congratulations! If the exercise worked and you got a clear "yes," you do not need to use any of the other methods provided for getting permission to find your purpose; they are alternative ways of achieving this same goal. It will probably help you a lot to read about them, though. If at this point, though, you're not interested in understanding more about your inner landscape, you can skip ahead to Chapter 5: Direct Access to Purpose.

Understanding Inner Protectors

The next method for creating permission to find your purpose takes an entirely different approach. It is much more complex than the previous exercise, but it also creates a tremendous amount of understanding of your internal landscape. You don't need to do this exercise and the previous one; you only need to create permission to find your purpose one way (as long as you do it thoroughly). If you are at all curious about how your psyche works, though, keep reading!

I keep referring to the ego as if it were one thing. It isn't. Your personality is composed of different sub-personalities, which are usually referred to as "voices," "selves," or "parts," depending on which psychological system you are using. These are like little people living inside your head. Think back on a time when you were trying to decide something with far-reaching consequences, like moving to another state or country, getting married or divorced, or taking or quitting an important job. Use a time when you were in a lot of confusion and conflict. You can probably remember an argument going on inside your head. Perhaps one part of you wanted to keep things the way they were or didn't want to take the risk to change. Another part may have wanted to go for it, to take the risk or make the commitment. It probably argued about the great things that would happen if you made the change, whatever it was.

This inner argument is a conflict between two or more of your parts, your sub-personalities. I said earlier that one of your ego's primary jobs is to keep you safe. These inner parts are the means by which it does that. Each of us has a small army of inner protectors, sub-personalities whose primary concern is our safety and well-being. They are constantly watching, keeping us out of danger, and trying to get our basic needs met.

At this point many people become concerned that I am describing multiple personality disorder. I am not. This is a description of a normal, healthy person. We all have multiple "personalities." What makes it a disorder is not the presence of these sub-personalities, but rather their unhealthy functioning. In a person with multiple personality disorder, there are sudden and dramatic switches between sub-personalities and forgetfulness about what occurred while in a different personality. In a psychologically healthy person, the presence and activities of the sub-personalities are relatively seamless and productive and therefore much more difficult to perceive.

It is important to get to know this internal cast of characters, because some of them may decide that knowing your purpose is too risky. If so, they will do their best to "protect" you by sabotaging your efforts to learn your purpose. This is extremely common. In fact, this is the primary obstacle most people face when seeking their purpose. Below are some of the common parts, the ones I encounter frequently in clients. There are many, many others, but these are the ones that most often sabotage attempts to connect to the soul.

THE PROTECTOR (OR CONTROLLER, OR RISK MANAGER)

This part is a kind of safety observer that keeps you from stepping in front of moving buses, betting your kids' college fund on a stock tip, or telling your boss to go pound sand. Most people have some version of this part, but it varies greatly in how powerful and visible it is. People who have a strong Protector seem less emotional and more logical. They take fewer risks, or take risks but calculate them carefully. While they often plan effectively, they may have difficulty being spontaneous or fun-loving.

People without an effective Protector part may take unnecessary chances, engaging in risky activities without sufficient planning and information. (This doesn't mean they don't have a Protector; it means the part isn't strong enough to keep them from taking excessive risks.)

THE CRITIC (OR JUDGE)

The Critic constantly tells you that you are ugly, stupid, fat, that you don't deserve love, that you'll never amount to anything, and so on. People with a strong Critic can appear different ways: They can be relentlessly critical of others, making them annoying and "anal"; they can be relentlessly critical of themselves, making them seem abused and victim-like; or they can do both behaviors. A person's Critic may be critical of themselves and of other people, at different times or even simultaneously. People with a strong Critic may find it difficult to complete tasks and projects, because it always has to be "perfect."

What most people don't understand is the value of this part. People with a very weak Critic often have trouble getting motivated, completing tasks, performing to high standards, and being ambitious. They make more mistakes than people with a stronger Critic. Most successful people have a powerful, active inner Critic. The Critic can inspire higher standards, higher ambition, and constant improvement; this is the usual goal of the Critic. Think of the U.S. Army slogan, "Be all you can be." The Critic is your ruthless inner personal trainer, trying to get you to be all you can be.

THE IMAGE CONSULTANT

If you're the kind of person who worries a lot about what others think of you, you have an active one of these. The Image Consultant pays close attention to how others react to you and it coaches you to behave appropriately. It usually censors your speech so you don't say anything that will give the wrong impression. A good Image Consultant can help you prepare for important meetings and stressful situations. It can coach you to dress for success, remember personal details about people, and say flattering things. The Image Consultant can also be seductive, even deceitful. Changing your presentation to match the needs and expectations of others has its downside. People with a very strong Image Consultant are so good at adapting to their "audience" that they may lose touch with their own identity.

People who do not have an effective Image Consultant part often make more social faux pas. (Think of the professor going to class with mismatched socks and bizarre-looking hair.) They may have difficulty with presentation-related activities like sales, marketing, job interviews, and politics.

THE SKEPTIC (OR DOUBTER, OR CYNIC)

You have probably heard a few comments from your inner Skeptic while reading this book! The Skeptic needs convincing and evidence. It is very alert to scams and unsupported product claims. People with an overly strong Skeptic can be difficult to convince of anything and may suffer from a lack of faith. They often assume the worst about people, believing that everyone is "working an angle" or trying to take advantage of them. Skeptics are very sensitive to inconsistencies and contradictions. People with a strong Skeptic may have a very limited spiritual life and, as a result, can suffer from a lack of fulfillment.

People without an effective Skeptic part can be very gullible. They are easy to take advantage of, susceptible to scams.

THE WOUNDED CHILD

The Wounded Child is different from the parts I've described so far. The previous parts are all protectors of one kind or another, responsible for keeping us safe. In fact, it's the inner Wounded Child that they're trying to protect. Here's how this works.

When we are babies, we naturally accept everything that comes our way. If we feel sad or hurt, we cry. If we're happy, we laugh. We reject none of our experiences. At some point we eventually encounter an experience that is too much for us. It is too painful to feel. We reject the experience and the feeling that it causes in us. We deny it: "This can't be happening. I won't feel this." More importantly, our psyche makes a decision to prevent it from ever happening to us again.

Let me give a specific example of how this works. Imagine that a baby boy is lying in his crib. He is hungry, and he cries out for his mother to come breast-feed him. His mother, meanwhile, is exhausted from caring for her infant and has elected to take a nap. It takes her 15 minutes to wake up and make it to the crib.

During this time, the baby boy has become terrified. His mother always responded immediately when he cried before. This time it is taking too long. He feels abandoned. This feeling of abandonment is too much for him. He rejects it. He must prevent her from abandoning him again.

When she is done breast-feeding him, she leaves to go finish her nap. He always falls asleep when she breast-feeds him. But this time he starts to cry as she heads for the door. He doesn't want her to go. He is trying to control his mother, to keep her from leaving.

This is an important moment, because the baby is now trying to control his environment. He begins to develop strategies to keep people from leaving. He notices that people smile when he makes baby noises, so he gurgles and waves his arms to keep them engaged so they will stay.

As a teenager, the boy has trouble ending relationships, even with people he doesn't like very much. He stays in touch with friends by email and phone after his family moves to another state. He learns to defuse conflict in groups so that no one will leave angry. He is good at identifying what others like and want, and he uses this information to keep them happy.

The important thing to notice about this scenario is that two things are happening simultaneously. The boy's future relationship challenges and psychological problems all have their root in this early wound. He is developing the "neuroses" that will plague him throughout his life. But his skills and abilities also have their root in this same event. He is developing the gifts that he will employ to relate to others and make a living. This process of wounding is neither "good" nor "bad"; it creates all of our gifts and all of our problems.

While your story is probably different from this example, somewhere in your past was a key event or circumstance that you experienced as a wound. In response to this wound, you adopted a strategy for dealing with life. Without it, you would still be lying in a crib, accepting whatever experiences come your way. You needed some experience that you could reject, some motive for trying to control your environment. If people were successful at creating a world in which no child ever felt bad, the generation that followed would be very unmotivated and without skills, if they were functional at all.

The Wounded Child is usually an unconscious part, so most people don't understand that it is present and influencing their behavior. However, it is the key to the structure of the psyche. It is the cornerstone on which the personality is built, because the protective parts (e.g., Protector, Critic, Image Consultant, and Skeptic) all develop to protect the Wounded Child. They are a defensive line, sent onto the field to prevent any more wounds from happening. Each one has its own position to play, its own way to prevent wounds. The Protector evaluates the chances that something bad will happen and coaches you to prepare for or avoid risky situations. The Critic harangues you to be perfect so that no one can ever criticize you. The Image Consultant evaluates other people and coaches you to behave in ways that will be acceptable. And the Skeptic keeps you from being taken advantage of by unscrupulous people and fraudulent organizations.

Let me say again that this is a simple and basic introduction to our inner landscape. We have literally hundreds of internal parts, but we usually only employ a few in our daily lives. There are beautiful, wonderful, creative parts. There are violent and aggressive parts. There are spiritual parts (more on that later). I have focused on the Wounded Child and its defensive team because these are the key obstacles in the search for purpose.

Reassuring Your Inner Protectors

Now that we've covered the basics of the Wounded Child and its team of inner protectors, we are ready to clear the way for direct access to purpose. These inner protectors are usually the ones that sabotage the search for purpose. Why? Because they perceive a direct connection to your soul and a full understanding of your purpose to be risky. This is the thing that most often prevents people from knowing their purpose: One or more of their protective parts has deemed it too great a risk. Having identified it as a risk, their protectors then sabotage any attempts they make to learn their purpose.

If the protectors can so easily sabotage the search for purpose, how will you ever learn it? What this means is that you will only be able to find your purpose if your protectors *believe it is in your best interests* to find your purpose. Furthermore, they must believe that it is in *their* best interests for you to find your purpose.

What do I mean by "*their* best interests"? Think of it this way: Your inner protectors have been influencing your life for decades. They make many of your key decisions. To a large extent, they are "in charge." If you discover your purpose, this could change. They could lose power.

So how do we get the protective parts on board so that we can proceed with our search? There are three ways we can do this:

1. Reassurance provided by this book
2. You conducting a dialogue with your parts
3. A trained facilitator conducting a dialogue with your parts

Reassurance provided by this book is the simplest and quickest way, so we will try that first. If it doesn't work, then you can try to dialogue with the parts on your own. If that doesn't work, you may need the help of a trained facilitator. (Remember, if you did the worst-case scenario exercise thoroughly, you may already have cleared a path through your ego. Working things out with your parts isn't always necessary.)

This next section is designed to directly address the concerns of your inner protectors. It is intended to address both their concerns about *your* safety and their concerns about *their* safety. (The parts are often concerned about what will happen to *them* if you make changes in your life.) It may provide them with enough of the information they need so that they will allow you to continue with your search for purpose. Please read the whole section.

REASSURING THE PROTECTOR

The Protector's main concern is ensuring that you will be safe. What your Protector needs to know is that you won't do anything crazy when you discover your purpose. The best thing you can do to reassure your Protector is to decide right now that you're going to take your time implementing your purpose and do it in a thoughtful and planned fashion. No one's purpose was ever served by running off half-cocked with inadequate planning and training. The Protector is a skilled planner and strategist. It can detect potential difficulties and avoid them. Give your Protector a chance to do its job while you are fulfilling your purpose, and you will be glad you did. I strongly recommend that you don't set about making life changes over the objections of your Protector.

REASSURING THE CRITIC

Critics are the hardest working and least appreciated part. They are responsible for much of our success, but they get no thanks for it. The best thing you can do is thank your Critic for motivating you to achieve the things you have done in your life. This doesn't mean that you want your Critic to continue harassing you, but the things you have to show for your life thus far are, at least in part, due to the hard work of your Critic.

Critics often hide the full extent of our gifts and abilities from us. The Critic needs to know that allowing you to fully express your gifts and power in the world doesn't mean you will become egotistical and arrogant or that you will no longer need it. You will still need it.

The best thing your Critic can do for you after you've found your purpose is to give you feedback about when you are out of alignment with your purpose. Think of the Critic as a coach or personal trainer. It may give you "tough love" at times, but your performance is your Critic's main concern. Finding your purpose will help you improve your performance, and this is usually appealing to the inner Critic.

REASSURING THE IMAGE CONSULTANT

Once you find your purpose, the next step is *not* to go shouting it from the rooftops. You need to exercise good judgment in choosing whom to tell about it. If you take your purpose to work, you will need to think carefully about how to translate your purpose into business language. A purpose statement in its raw form rarely belongs on a web-site, resume, or business card. Once you find your purpose, you will need your Image Consultant to help you decide whom to tell and what to say. You may also need its help to market and sell a new purpose-related venture, service, or product. It will help your Image Consultant if you commit to keeping your newfound purpose to yourself, until it seems wise and productive to share it with others.

REASSURING THE SKEPTIC

Unfortunately, there is no conclusive way to prove the existence of a soul or a life purpose. We are operating in the realms of belief and faith, not science. Fortunately, there are a number of ways to verify that what occurred was "real," that you actually connected to your soul and that what you received is really your purpose. If this happens, you will need your Skeptic to help you make this determination. Your Skeptic's role also will be to decide whether the things you choose to believe pose any danger to you, not whether they are "true" in some objective way. We'll talk more about that once we have information from your soul to work with. It is not necessary to have absolute proof to decide whether a purpose has value or not. The ultimate test comes when you try living from your new purpose. If it really is your purpose, the difference it makes in your life will be obvious. If it does work, does it matter whether it was really your soul talking or not? What if you were to spend the rest of your life happy, successful, and fulfilled, but never quite sure whether you really *knew* this was your purpose? Would that be such a bad thing?

Take a breath and notice what you are feeling. If the reassurance worked, you will feel calmer, more ready to know your purpose. This means that your parts are less agitated, more acclimated to the idea of you finding your purpose. If this is what you are feeling, then go ahead and attempt the self-study methods in Chapter 6. If you have lingering fears, anxieties, or concerns, you should proceed with the next section to negotiate with your parts. If you proceed without doing the negotiating and the self-study methods don't work, come back and do the next section to clear your remaining ego blocks.

Negotiating with Inner Protectors

If your protective parts are not satisfied, your next step is to have a direct dialogue with them. Our goal is to get permission from each one to find your purpose. If you do not have permission from one of your parts, none of the direct access methods will work. Negotiating with your parts one-by-one can be time consuming, but it creates a more thorough form of permission than the worst-case scenario exercise we did earlier. Even if you did that exercise thoroughly, it is wise to check for any parts that might get in the way of finding your purpose. This gives a much higher degree of certainty that we have cleared a path through the ego.

Unless you are a certified hypnotherapist or a trained Voice Dialogue facilitator, the best way to do this is using a method called active imagination. Carl Jung, one of the founders of modern psychology, first conceived of the process of active imagination. He envisioned it as a means for the conscious mind to engage and communicate with the unconscious. Active imagination can be used both to clear ego blocks and to find your purpose. Right now, you will use it only to clear ego blocks.

Active imagination can be done in many different ways, including painting, sculpture, dance, and visualization. We will use its written form. Basically, active imagination entails role-playing the different parts involved in the communication. In this case, the players will be you and any of your inner protectors who have concerns about you knowing your purpose.

The interaction is conducted in much the same way as a play is written, that is, each part is named and then its lines are written. This is critically important; if you do not write down the names of the different parts, then you are conducting a monologue, not a dialogue. In most cases, you don't need to do anything else to get it to work; it's just that simple. When done properly, it might look something like this:

Suzie:	I'd like to talk to my inner Skeptic.
Skeptic:	*What do you want?*
Suzie:	I'm interested in finding my purpose. Do you have any concerns about that?
Skeptic:	*Of course I do! This whole thing seems pretty far-fetched to me. In fact, this active imagination thing has got to be some kind of gimmick. How do you know you aren't just making it all up?*

> Suzie: I'm not sure, this is the first time I've tried it. You do
>   sound a lot like a Skeptic, though.
>
> Skeptic: *I suppose that's true...*

There's nothing special going on here; Suzie is just writing down both sides of the conversation. Using this method, you can now begin to talk to and negotiate with any parts of you that are having concerns about you finding your purpose. You don't need to know in advance which part it is; you can just ask for a part that is having concerns, then ask which part it is. It can come up with a name for itself.

Once you've opened up a dialogue with a part, your goal is to obtain its permission to find your purpose. The part may have concerns about what will happen to you or other people you care about. It may also have concerns about what will happen to it! It's important when negotiating with a part to hear and address its concerns fully, not just try to strong-arm it or convince it. The grudging permission you might get will not serve you in finding and living your purpose.

The first step is to engage the part in a conversation. Having made contact, find out about the part and what role it plays in you. Learn about its goals and needs. Once you have a clear sense of the part and how it operates in you, ask it about its concerns. Don't argue with it; just ask questions to understand its reservations. If you were just doing general journaling, it would make sense for you to speculate about the nature of the issue. Since you're having a two-way dialogue, the right move is to ask. Start with open-ended questions that elicit information. Do your best to leave your judgments, preferences, and agenda out of the way for this phase.

Once you have a clear understanding of what its concerns are, try to negotiate with the part to see what it would need in order to allow you to find your purpose. Some things that often work for parts when negotiating for permission to find your purpose are:

✓ Respect and appreciation from you

✓ Acknowledgment of how the part has served you in your life to date

✓ Your permission to veto your plan to implement your purpose later

✓ Clarity about what support you will need from the part after you find your purpose (the parts usually don't want to lose their jobs!)

First, read the example below. Then do the exercise. Your experience will probably not be anything like the example; just keep asking questions and looking for a win-win solution for you and the part!

Example

Caroll Schwartz is a mentor in the Purposeful Coach Certification Program. She is one of the leaders of the Purposeful Coach Community, an organization of thousands of coaches who are learning life purpose methods. Sandy is a client of Caroll's. Here is a dialogue Sandy had in active imagination with a part that had concerns about her finding her purpose. Notice that initially she doesn't know which part she's talking to, so she just writes "Part" until she figures out its name.

Sandy:	*I would like to talk to a part of me that doesn't think it is a good idea that I know my purpose. Would you please identify yourself?*
Part:	*I'm the Caregiver. You are going to be disappointed and regret the process of finding your purpose.*
Sandy:	*Why do you think that?*
Caregiver:	*When you gave up teaching high school and took that Financial Planning job, you nearly starved to death. Didn't you learn anything from that?*

Sandy: Yes, but that was different. I didn't try to find my
            purpose; I just made a career change into another
            industry. I agree it was not as fulfilling or easy
            as I thought it would be. But if you look at the big
            picture, it was very useful in my development. I
            probably never would be in my current comfortable
            situation if I had not learned about investing and
            risk tolerance in that job.

Caregiver: *Exactly! You are comfortable and on track for
            retirement. Are you going to throw that away and
            start over?*

Sandy: Not necessarily. I want to know my purpose for
            personal growth. I think part of the reason the
            Financial Planning job was not a success is that it
            wasn't something that was my purpose. It was only
            a stepping stone of knowledge.

Caregiver: *Why will this be different?*

Sandy: It will be different because if I know my purpose,
            I have to be good at it. Why else would it be my
            purpose? If I promise to consult you, my Caregiver,
            and whomever else comes forward, before I take
            any new direction, would that be agreeable to you?

Caregiver: *You're always pushing us to agree.*

Sandy: Okay, if I promise to consult prior to going forward, will
            you consent to letting me find my purpose?

Caregiver: *No, No, No!*

Sandy: Why not?

Caregiver: *You will regret the move and blame us. We will live with
            your regret and unhappiness.*

Sandy:	First of all, I don't think my life purpose will be so traumatic that I can't incorporate a part of it, if not all of it, into my everyday life. Since I don't know what it is, I can't be more specific. What assurances can I give you to allow me to pursue knowing my purpose?
Caregiver:	*You received a perfectly good contact to set you up for a job interview.*
Sandy:	Yes, but it was for an Inventory Analyst job in manufacturing. I can't bear to think about going back to that field.

This is what often happens when people first try to negotiate with parts. Sandy is working hard to convince the part, and the part is resisting. What she needs to do is hear more about the part's concerns and find ways to help allay those concerns. This will require more questioning, more listening, and less convincing. Let's see what happened when she picked up the conversation again the next morning.

Sandy:	Good morning, Caregiver. I have done some thinking about what you said yesterday. You bring out some good points. After all, you <u>are</u> my caregiver. Why do you call yourself "Caregiver"? Are you taking care of me? What does that mean?
Caregiver:	*Others look out for you. I have to pick up the pieces when you run astray. You do things that sabotage your success. You go off on tangents.*
Sandy:	I respect your advice and <u>do</u> want to hear your concerns. Your job at picking up the pieces and nursing me back to "health" will be easier on <u>both</u> of us if we collaborate and come up with a plan. Deal?

Caregiver: *Okay.*

Sandy: Here is what I was thinking. Jump in if you disagree
              or have more to add. Assuming you and the other
              parts will agree to let me know my life purpose, I put
              together a mission statement, if you will: "I want to
              obtain a position that will bring out the best in me,
              further align me with my life purpose, and meet my
              financial goals." Please notice that I said, "further
              align me with my life purpose," not take off blindly
              and fulfill it. I respect your concerns and take
              them to heart. You know my previous career was not
              healthy for me. You are my Caregiver and felt the
              rapid heartbeats and despairing feelings while I
              positioned myself for escape. I was very responsible
              in my planning. You know that. I am sure you and my
              other parts were my internal guides. Now I am free
              and able to think about other possibilities.

Caregiver: *What else will you promise?*

Sandy: It seems the financial part is your biggest concern.
              I put a few statistics together and want to run them
              by you. If I promise to put away $10,000 each year
              ($833.33 per month), I should still be on target
              to retire at 62, if I want to. The way I look at it,
              my horse was costing me about $700-$800 and I
              always made the payment for her, even when I was
              a Financial Planner and really hurting for money. At
              $100,000 income, it is 10%; at $50,000 income, it
              is 20%. I think it would be hard at 20%, but I could
              do it. What I am saying is that I commit to $10,000
              per year into retirement as my stated goal. Having

said that, it is clear I can't accept any job under $50,000 even to start over.

Caregiver: *That's too low for the way you want to live.*

Sandy: I agree it is rock bottom, but I may need to start low to get in the door. The bottom is not my goal, just my safety net. Agreed?

Caregiver: *I guess.*

Sandy: I commit to you to save $10,000 per year for retirement. I commit to consult you and the other parts before taking any job or going in any unexpected direction that might derail my retirement goals. Will you consent to let me know my life purpose?

Caregiver: *Yes.*

Sandy: Will you further consent to make me aware of any other concerns as we go along? This is new for me, too. I need your guidance and welcome your input. Thank you for the care you have shown me over the years. I am happy to meet you and want to grow to love you. Your work is not over and I will stumble, I am sure. Please work with me to succeed. You are a trusted advisor. Thank you.

Sandy has received permission from her Caregiver part. She is still doing most of the talking, but she is also taking the concerns of the part more seriously than she did the first time. Provided she sticks to her agreements, the part will probably be willing to step aside and let her find her purpose.

Exercise: Getting Permission from Parts

Okay, your turn. This is a chance to see whether there are any parts of you that are not on board with finding your purpose. You will use the same back-and-forth active imagination dialogue as in the example above. If you're not sure which part of you has concerns, there are two ways you can go: 1) You can do what Sandy did and just ask for a part, or 2) you can work with each of the "usual suspects": the Protector, Critic, Image Consultant, Skeptic, and the Wounded Child. Either way, before you consider yourself complete, check to see whether any other parts have concerns about you finding your purpose.

The dialogue goes through phases. There are different questions and techniques that work for each phase.

Phase I: Establish Communication

1.   Open to a blank page in your journal or open up a new computer document.

2.   Write your name, followed by a colon (":"), and then ask for a part that has concerns about finding your purpose. You can ask for a specific part by name, or you can just ask for any part that has concerns to come forward.

3.   Write the part's name, followed by a colon (":"). If you don't know which part it is, just write "Part" for the name.

4.   Now write an answer. Just write whatever comes to mind; don't worry if you feel like you're making it up.

Phase II: Learn about the Part

5.   This is the stage where you learn about the part and the role it plays in you. Don't ask about your purpose or its concerns just

yet. Once you know what it would like to be called, write that in front of its answers, instead of writing "Part" for its name.

6. Here are some good questions you can try asking:

    a. "What should I call you?"

    b. "What role do you play in me? In my life?"

    c. "What are your goals?"

    d. "What are your needs?"

    e. "When did you first appear in me?"

    f. "Are you modeled after someone in my life?"

7. If you can find it in your heart to do so, it is helpful at this stage to express appreciation for the role the part has played in your life. If you've asked enough questions, you should be able to see that the part is trying to act in your best interests, even if you don't like how it's doing its role.

Phase III: Learn about Its Concerns

8. In this stage, your task is to learn as much as possible about any concerns the part has about you finding your purpose. It's important not to try to solve or resolve any problems it raises; just keep asking questions. Here are some good ones to ask:

    a. "What concerns do you have about me finding my purpose?"

    b. "What would happen if those concerns actually came true?"

    c. "If it were up to you, would you keep me from finding my purpose? Why or why not?"

9. If you want to be really thorough, you can do the worst-case scenario exercise with the part. Just like in the exercise, ask it:

a. "What's the worst thing that could happen if your fear came true?"

b. "What's the worst thing that could happen if *that* came true?" Keep asking this question, over and over.

c. When the part starts to repeat itself or can't think of anything worse, ask, "If this starts to happen, at what point should I stop pursuing my purpose?"

d. Write down whatever constraints the part gives you.

Phase IV: Negotiate

10. This is the critical step. Now that you know the nature of the part's fears, you can negotiate with it. It's important that you don't argue with the part or try to convince it that everything will be okay. You must take the part's concerns seriously in order for this to work. Here are some good questions you can ask during this phase:

a. "What would you need in order to give me permission to find my purpose?"

b. "What agreements can we make to ensure that your concerns don't come to pass?" If you did the worst-case scenario exercise with the part, you can make agreements about the constraints the part wrote down.

c. "What role would you like to play after I find my purpose?"

11. If you need to make promises and commitments in order to get permission, don't make any promises you're not willing to keep. Write them down somewhere so you can keep track of them.

Phase V: Wrap-up

12. Once you have permission from this part, restate whatever agreements or promises you've made with it. Find out whether and when the part needs you to check in with it again.

13. If you've been unable to get permission to find your purpose, ask the part what it recommends you do next.

14. Thank the part, even if it didn't give you permission.

15. When you're complete with this session, transfer any agreements or commitments you've made to places where you can keep track of them, like your to-do list or calendar. If you do not keep your agreements, the part will probably sabotage your attempts to find your purpose.

Congratulations! Now repeat the process with another part. Keep doing this until no parts come forward with objections to you finding your purpose. This will likely take you at least several sessions to complete.

IF YOU DO NOT GET PERMISSION FROM ANY ONE PART, DON'T GO ANY FURTHER. Thank it and don't try the direct access methods yet. If you "push" a part that is saying "no," it could shut down your ability to use the direct access methods altogether. You can either try again another time or hire a professional to help you. (See the next section on facilitated methods for clearing a path through the ego.)

Before we move on, I want to highlight some interesting side effects that come from using this method. Unless you have done "parts" work previously in another setting, this approach will open up a vast inner world to you. Most people are blissfully (or miserably) unaware that they have parts and that the parts usually aren't getting along all that well. By establishing communication with your parts, you can learn invaluable information about how your psyche works and even make improvements! This goes for "bad" parts as well; every part, no matter how much you dislike it, exists to serve you in some way. Separately from getting permission to find your purpose, talking to your parts regularly can help you make better decisions, take action more whole-heartedly (or "whole-partedly"), and experience the beauty and glory of your inner landscape.

Facilitated Methods for Clearing Ego Blocks

If negotiating with your inner protectors still hasn't quieted your concerns, then you may need to engage a facilitator to help you clear your ego blocks. There are a number of different facilitated techniques for dealing with parts, including Voice Dialogue, neuro-linguistic programming (NLP), hypnotherapy, gestalt therapy, and Internal Family Systems therapy (IFS). You can read more about these methods in the chapters on Voice Dialogue and hypnotherapy later in the book. A practitioner skilled in any of these methods can assist you in clearing a path through the ego by negotiating directly with your parts on your behalf.

There are many other methods you can use as well. Two that deal with limiting beliefs rather than fears and parts are the Lefkoe Method and Lion Goodman's "Belief Closet" method. Both are forms of guided meditation that give you an opportunity to remove limiting beliefs. They require facilitation because often the beliefs that are limiting you are unconscious. Clearing all of your limiting beliefs about finding and living your purpose has the same effect as addressing your fears.

Additional methods that can be used to clear fears and limiting beliefs include the Emotional Freedom Techniques (EFT), the Tapas Acupressure Technique (TAT), the Sedona Method, and Eye Movement Desensitization and Reprocessing (EMDR). Any one of these could clear a path to your purpose after a few sessions with a trained practitioner. No doubt there are many other techniques that I am unfamiliar with.

A final word on other methods for clearing a path through the ego: There are many oversimplified techniques for dealing with fears that will not work. Anything that minimizes, overrides, suppresses, or dishonors your fears will drive them into the unconscious and make finding your purpose that much more difficult. For example, a gung-ho, "just do it" approach to overcoming your fears will not work. Neither will treating the parts that have concerns as "gremlins" that need to be ignored, disempowered, or removed. The human psyche is a complex and beautiful organism; each part of you is there for a reason, whether you personally like it or not. Treat your parts, your fears, and your beliefs with respect as you seek to change them. You will be glad you did.

> *"The secret of success is constancy of purpose."*
>
> – Benjamin Disraeli

Chapter Five

Direct Access to Purpose

How Direct Access Works

Direct access methods are far more accurate for identifying life purpose than indirect access methods. Since the soul is the part of you that already knows your purpose, having your soul directly disclose it to you gives the least subjective, most clear expression of your purpose possible. Think of this like running a telephone wire from one floor to another. A person on the top floor of a house would like to have a conversation with a person in the basement. Shouting does little good, but running a telephone wire from the top floor down to the basement will solve the problem.

All direct access methods share this two-way line of communication between the ego and the soul. Using this two-way communication link, the ego asks questions and the soul answers them. The questions need not be restricted to life purpose, which makes these methods extremely useful for answering any question that is plaguing you.

Let me draw an important distinction here: I am *not* talking about using a psychic or channeler to find your purpose. In those methods, another living human being tells you what your purpose is. In the direct methods we will use, your soul will tell you directly what your purpose is. This eliminates the concern that the psychic or channeler got it wrong. It also means that you can talk to your soul whenever you like, without having to set up a session with a psychic.

The reason that there are so many direct access methods is because there are many different ways of establishing this connection. Each method is a different way of getting the ego into a state where it is capable of asking questions and receiving answers from the soul. Unlike indirect access methods, not all direct access methods work for all people. The individual methods have different rates of success as well.

Furthermore, while indirect access methods work for people who have most any belief system, this is not true of direct access methods. Some direct access methods may be uncomfortable for some people, or may fall outside of the confines of their belief system or faith. Therefore, it is appropriate to have a number of different direct access methods from which to choose. You will need to read about and evaluate the different methods. Select the ones that are most likely to work for you and most closely match your belief system.

The direct access methods are divided into two categories: self-study methods and facilitated methods. The self-study methods are ones that you can do on your own. It makes sense for you to start here because you can get the answers more quickly and will not have to hire someone in order to learn your life's purpose. The facilitated methods require the assistance of someone with specific expertise. Each of the facilitated methods requires some form of training.

I recommend that you read about each of the self-study methods first and choose the ones that feel and seem most appropriate for you. Try each of these methods and see if you are able to create a connection with your soul. You only need one method to work in order to find your purpose! Once you find a method that works, you can continue to use it to get whatever information you need. If you are unable to create a connection to your soul using any of the self-study methods, consider using the facilitated methods.

Trusted Sources

So now we've cleared the fears and concerns that block access to your purpose. Since we'll be using direct access methods, we need to connect directly to someone or something that already knows your purpose. But what does that mean? To whom or what will we connect?

In setting up any two-way communication, it is important to know to whom you're talking. Returning to the telephone metaphor, we are about to try to place a call and to get answers to some very important questions. Whom are you going to call? This is the place in the book where your personal psychological, spiritual, and religious belief systems matter the most. I've been using the term "soul" very loosely to describe the part of you that knows your purpose. Now, it is time to get much more specific.

The basic question is this: Whom or what will you trust to answer questions about your purpose? To designate whom or what you're going to call, I will use the term "trusted source." "Trusted source" means just that. Whom or what do you trust to answer these questions?

In order to qualify as a trusted source, something or someone needs to meet three criteria. You must believe that:

1. It exists.

2. It already knows your purpose.

3. It is capable of communicating with you.

You don't need to be absolutely certain about these things. You could believe that something might exist, might know your purpose, and might be able to communicate it to you. This can be sufficient (though being more certain is helpful).

We're talking about something divine or transpersonal, not a living person. I don't know your purpose! (Neither do your living parents, children, or spouse, even if they insist that they do.) What, in your universe, already knows your purpose? This is the key question! Until you answer this question, you won't know whom to ask! Having a name or label for your trusted source is important; think of it like a phone number. It's hard to make a call unless you know whom you're trying to reach.

There are three basic types of trusted sources: internal, universal, and personal. You may have any or all of these types of trusted sources.

INTERNAL SOURCES

An "internal" trusted source is some aspect of your psyche that knows your purpose. It is called "internal" because you view this as a part of yourself. Where we draw the line between ourselves and the rest of reality is somewhat arbitrary. Recall that one of the functions of the ego is to preserve your sense of self, your individual identity. It does this by establishing and maintaining this line, by declaring certain things to be "me" and everything else to be "not me."

Some people will be comfortable only with internal trusted sources. This is often true of people who are atheistic, agnostic, and/or strongly mentally oriented. For some of these people, it is challenging and uncomfortable for the ego to acknowledge powerful or divine forces outside of themselves. That's fine; look inward. Do you believe that some part of you is divine? Is there some source of deeper wisdom or intuition within you? Can you accept, even hypothetically, that some part of you already knows your purpose, and has known it all along? If so, what would you call this part of you? Some typical terms used to name internal trusted sources are "soul," "spirit," "higher self," "Buddha nature," and "entelechy."

Remember, in order to qualify as a trusted source, you must believe that it exists, it knows your purpose, and it can communicate with you. Here is how one client described his internal trusted source: "Do I believe that some part of me already knows my purpose? I suppose that could be true. I sometimes feel that something deep inside me is guiding me in some way. I don't really have a name for it, but 'soul' is as good a name as any. If I do have a soul, it would definitely know my purpose. Could it communicate with me? Sure, I suppose so, though that's never really happened in any kind of direct way. It would be nice if it did, though maybe a little spooky."

Note that this man doesn't have a strong belief in his soul, but it is sufficient to use direct access methods. His belief system allows for his soul to exist, to know his purpose, and to communicate his purpose to him.

If you have an internal trusted source, take a moment and write down the name you use for it. Don't worry about what anyone else calls it; just write down the name that feels right to you.

In addition to looking inward for trusted sources, you can also look outward. There may be external trusted sources in your universe. External trusted sources come in two types: universal and personal.

UNIVERSAL SOURCES

A trusted source is universal if you believe that it knows (or would know) everyone's purpose, not just yours. Some common names people use for universal trusted sources are God, Jesus, the Universe, Source, and Spirit. Universal trusted sources work well for monotheists (e.g., Christians, Jews, Muslims, and Bahá'ís), but poorly for agnostics and atheists.

Here's an example of how a Christian client chose her universal trusted source: "Well, of course I believe in God. And yes, God knows everyone's purpose; He has to. I'm not really comfortable communicating directly with God, though. But the Holy Spirit talks to people; I could learn my purpose from the Holy Spirit."

Note that for this client, though God exists and knows her purpose, she's not *allowed* to talk directly to Him. That's fine; choose an intermediary. Who could communicate your purpose to you on God's behalf? Jesus? The Holy Spirit? Mother Mary?

Is there a universal trusted source in your universe? What deity or entity in your belief system knows everyone's purpose? Write down the name of your universal trusted source, if any.

PERSONAL SOURCES

Personal trusted sources are another kind of external trusted source. A personal trusted source is something or someone that you believe has a special, personal interest in your purpose (but not everyone else's). Do you believe that someone or something watches over you? Examples of personal trusted sources are a guardian angel, a guide, a spirit animal, or a loved one who has died.

Remember, in order to qualify as a trusted source, you must believe that it exists, knows your purpose, and is capable of communication. Here's how a coach I trained described her personal trusted source: "I know my husband is still with me; I can feel his presence. He wants me to live my purpose."

Do you have a guide, a dead loved one, or a guardian angel? Does something watch over you? Do you believe it knows your purpose? Write down the name(s) of any personal trusted source(s) you believe in.

Vague concepts don't make good trusted sources. We're looking for an active, sentient agency. "Life" would qualify as a trusted source if you believe Life to be a self-aware force with a plan. If you believe that everyone matters and ought to be nice to one another and call that personal value "Life," then "Life" probably isn't a sufficiently specific being or force to qualify as a trusted source. It needs to be something that could answer your questions, which a principle or idea can't do.

For those who are neither religious nor spiritual, the appropriate place to look for a trusted source is psychology. Most people don't find it hard to accept that they have an unconscious. If you believe you have an unconscious, you can probably entertain, if only for the sake of argument, the idea that within your unconscious is some aspect of your psyche that knows your purpose. This is what I have been referring to as a "soul." If you're uncomfortable with the term "soul," the term "entelechy" works well. This word was originally coined by the Greek philosopher Aristotle. It refers to an organism's innate perfection, its impulse to growth and development, its instinct to manifest to its fullest potential. Your entelechy, then, is the part of you that knows your purpose and is seeking to manifest it through you. It is unnecessary to attach any religious significance to this. You can view it in the same way you view your inner Critic or Skeptic, just another part of you with a specific function to perform. The only difference is that it's probably unconscious: You may have no clear sense of this part of you, while you may be very aware of your skeptical and critical thoughts.

If you've been keeping a list, it's pretty common to have 2-3 trusted sources written down at this point. This is fine, but you only need one for the direct access methods to work! Pick the one that seems most comfortable for you and start with it. If that doesn't work, you can try another one.

If you have no trusted sources written down, then direct access methods may not work for you. Perhaps you believe that you have no innate purpose, that nothing is predetermined. Simply declare your purpose! What meaning would you like to create in the world? How would you like your life to be remembered? Choose some lofty goal, something that will stretch your abilities, and pursue it wholeheartedly. Give this book to someone else who believes they have an innate purpose.

It is also possible not to identify your trusted source by name. In effect, this means inviting any entity or agency that is capable of answering questions about your purpose to do so. For the sake of convenience, it usually works to ask the agency or entity what it wishes to be called. This is helpful if you wish to repeat the direct access method in the future to gain more information. A caution, though: Your chances of using direct access methods successfully are reduced if you try to work without naming a specific trusted source.

Remember, selection of your trusted source is a highly personal decision. I recommend against allowing yourself to be influenced by others in this choice. It doesn't matter what you were taught in Sunday school when you were a child or what your friends and family think you believe. Be honest with yourself. What do *you* really believe? Only you can determine who or what you should be asking about your purpose. If you use somebody else's beliefs, it just won't work.

Asking Good Questions

Now you know where you will go to ask questions, your trusted source. You also need to know what questions you're going to ask. So long as you understand these three aspects well enough, it will be simple to ask your trusted source about them:

1. "What is my essence?"

2. "What is my blessing?"

3. "What is my mission?"

These were defined in Chapter 2: What Does Purpose Look Like? Recall that your purpose is the sum of these three things, so it doesn't make sense to ask, "What is my purpose?" These three questions will probably be plenty for your first time out; don't try to get everything resolved at once!

The answers you get in your first session will likely require clarification, so feel free to ask follow-up questions. In particular, it makes sense to ask a bunch of questions to fully understand your blessing and mission. It usually takes several interactions with a trusted source to get all these questions answered.

CLARIFYING YOUR BLESSING

Since your blessing is a process that you have been designed to do, you should ask enough questions to fully understand this process. This will typically take place over a series of interactions with your trusted source, not just one. Here are the questions I recommend asking:

- ✓ "What is my blessing?"
- ✓ "For whom is it intended? In what state are people when they need my blessing?"
- ✓ "What are the steps of my blessing? What happens first, second, third, etc.?"
- ✓ "When does it end? How do I know when I'm finished?"
- ✓ "What effect does it have on people? In what state are they when my blessing is complete?"

Knowing when to stop is a very important feature of the blessing. You can make yourself miserable if you are unaware of your blessing and continue past the end of the process. My college roommate's father was a gifted leader and entrepreneur. His blessing expressed itself with distressed companies; he was a turnaround expert. Startups that were failing would hire him as CEO, and the results were pure magic. Within months of coming on board, he had fired the problem people, set a new course for the company, and things would be moving forward beautifully. But once things were going well, problems began. He would continue to reorganize and shift things around, and the company would have difficulty settling into a rhythm. Within a few years, his influence began to be a negative one. Several times he was fired by company owners or venture capitalists.

Had he fully understood his blessing, he would have known when to leave. He could have told the owners that they would need him for about two years, but then they would have to find someone else to replace him. The transition could have taken place amicably, and everyone would have been served by it.

CLARIFYING YOUR MISSION

If you have a mission, it can be challenging to understand it completely. Trusted sources are often reluctant to reveal the details of your mission, and your ego probably will feel daunted and overwhelmed by it. Nonetheless, it is critically important to grasp as much of your mission as you can, so that you can make informed choices about it. You can do some of it, all of it, or none of it, but you can't choose unless you know what it is. Here are some questions I recommend asking to get a good sense of your mission. Again, this will probably happen over the course of several interactions with your trusted source, not just one.

- ✓ "What is my mission?"
- ✓ "What problem in the world have I been created to solve?"
- ✓ "Which group of people have I been sent to serve?"
- ✓ "What change in the world have I been designed to make?"
- ✓ "Given all of the ways I could use my blessing and all of the people I could serve with it, in which ways and with which groups of people would it be most purposeful for me to use it?"
- ✓ "How do I get started with my mission?"

Taken together, these questions should give you plenty of information about your purpose. Trusted sources can reveal lots of other things, too, in addition to your purpose. But what else can you ask?

While trusted sources are highly informed on some matters that to the ego are very opaque, they will generally only answer certain types of questions. Trusted sources are strategists. They think big picture, in terms of an entire lifetime, rather than in terms of individual events or choices. As a result, while your trusted source might be very willing to answer questions about your life purpose, asking it questions about what you want for lunch or what color of car to buy are completely irrelevant from its point of view. This kind of detailed question will tend to either elicit no answer or confusion. Try to stick to big-picture questions about events in your life and about your growth and development. These are the things your trusted source cares about the most and the things it is most qualified to advise you about.

It does make sense to ask your trusted source questions about critical choices that you're facing. For example, taking or leaving a job, a marriage, moving, or other things that significantly influence the course of your life. Avoid asking questions about predicting the future. Trusted sources don't view time in the same way we do. They aren't particularly interested in giving you stock tips or telling you who is going to win the next election. Remember, trusted sources are concerned with your growth and development. Understanding explicit details about the future is unlikely to help you grow and manifest into the person you're most meant to be. It does make sense to ask trusted sources questions about who you're becoming, who you're developing into, and how to facilitate that process.

Avoid yes-no and multiple choice questions. Open-ended questions work best. "What do you recommend? What counsel do you have?" Obviously, in seeking your life purpose, it makes sense to ask questions about your essence, blessing, and mission. Having a firm grasp of these concepts will enable you to ask good questions about them and to understand your trusted source's responses. Your trusted source may flatly refuse to answer certain questions. This is normal. Trusted sources are very selective about what information they reveal and concerned about the effect that information will have on you. If your trusted source deems that you are not ready to know something, it will not disclose it. From your trusted source's point of view, the question is this: "Will knowing this information help you to develop and manifest purposefully?" If the answer is "no," the information will not be revealed. Trusted sources deal on a "need to know" basis. This means that certain information that is not available now may become available later. Think of it as a matching funds program. If your trusted source gives you instructions and you follow them, then it will likely give you more instructions and information later. If your trusted source gives you information and instructions and you ignore them, usually, no more information will be forthcoming in later sessions.

When you engage in a dialogue with your trusted source, don't lecture it. You are there to ask questions and to record the answers. Remember, you get to choose what to do with the answers. Just because your trusted source gave you an instruction, it doesn't mean you have to do it. Now it's time to write down some of the things you would like to get advice about from your trusted source.

Exercise: Create Your Question List

It will be useful to have your list of questions ready before your first attempt to contact a trusted source. Trying to think of them on the spot can be distracting and take you out of the experience.

Go ahead and write the title "Questions" on a blank piece of paper or computer document. The first three questions should be:

1. "What is my essence?"

2. "What is my blessing?"

3. "What is my mission?"

Okay, now write down 3-5 additional questions. Make sure they are open-ended questions about issues facing you in your life: problems or decisions at work, at school, or in relationships. Keep this question list handy; you'll need it when you start using the direct methods!

> *"The spiritual journey is the unlearning of fear and prejudices and the acceptance of love back in our hearts."*
>
> – Marianne Williamson

Chapter Six

Self-Study Methods

At this point, you should have a clear understanding of the difference between ego and soul, and you should have done some clearing of your fears and ego blocks. You know who your trusted source is, and you know the questions you want to ask it. Now you are ready for the fun part, establishing the connection to your trusted source.

I recommend you try all of the self-study methods before you use any of the facilitated methods. If you can learn your purpose on your own, why would you want to hire a professional? For this reason I have put the self-study methods first. Methods 3-6 each have an exercise you can do on your own.

You may find that when you read the description of a method, you feel a strong resistance to using it. I recommend that you honor this resistance and move on to another method. If you find yourself unwilling to use any of the self-study methods, you probably need to do some more work clearing ego blocks. Try the *Negotiating with Inner Protectors* exercise in Chapter 4: Clearing a Path through the Ego.

I recommend that you read the descriptions of all four self-study methods first, then choose the one you are most drawn to. Use it first, following the instructions carefully. If it works, you're done! There is no need to try a second method. Of all of the direct access methods, you only need one to work in order to find your purpose. If one doesn't work, move on to another self-study method. As I said, try all of them before you attempt any of the facilitated methods. You only need to use a facilitated method if none of the self-study methods work.

Method 3: Prayer

Prayer is the simplest and most direct method of establishing a line of communication with your trusted source, which is why I have placed it first. When it works, it can be a source of guidance, information, strength, and serenity. Once established, this channel is usually available thereafter, and people can use it again and again to gain fresh insight and be reminded of their purpose.

Most prayer is not intended to be two-way communication. People pray all the time without expecting to hear answers: They pray for healing, to give thanks, for loved ones, and for peace. What distinguishes prayer as a method for finding your purpose is that when you pray, you ask a question and then you *wait for a response*. Many people experience having their prayers answered later, through events and the words and actions of other people. This is not what I'm talking about. When it works, this method results in direct, immediate, two-way communication with your trusted source, usually in words.

This method is most likely to work for you if you already pray. It works best for people who hear answers when they pray. It relies heavily on your faith in your religious and spiritual beliefs. Prayer works best with universal trusted sources, such as God. Most people wouldn't pray to their own soul or to their dead father. If you don't have a universal trusted source, you may find yourself uncomfortable with the prospect of prayer. If so, move on and try a different method.

You may have prayed thousands of times already without hearing a response. Why should this time be any different? Two reasons: First, you may not have tried two-way prayer before. Second, even if you did, you probably didn't clear your ego's fears and blocks before you tried it! Most people don't hear direct answers when they pray, even after clearing their ego blocks, so don't stress about it if nothing happens. Give it a try. If it doesn't work, move on to another method.

Exercise: Prayer

I've made these instructions very general; feel free to modify them to make the process more compatible with your religious or spiritual beliefs and practices. Once you become accustomed to two-way communication in prayer, you will probably find that it requires far less setup than I have described here. People who are practiced at this can do it at work, on a bus, or even in the middle of a meeting! Imagine pausing for a moment during a job interview to get some quick advice from God...

Don't worry about whether you are "making it up." Some skeptical response is natural after establishing a direct connection. Some part of you will usually chime in and start questioning whether what you heard or felt was "real." This is much more likely to happen if this is the first time you have received responses during prayer. If you have heard answers many times, you are less likely to have a skeptical response. Ask your inner Skeptic to wait until after the exercise is over; we will evaluate whether it worked or not in Chapter 8: Interpreting Your Results.

1. Create quiet, private space and time for yourself. It is best to do this at a time when you are not concerned with pressing deadlines or other distractions. Have a journal and pen handy.

2. Direct your thoughts to your trusted source. Ask, "Are you there?"
    Answers may come as words, images, memories, feelings, or direct
    knowing. For now, assume that anything that happens immedi-
    ately after you ask a question is an answer.

3. If you hear or feel a response, check for permission: "Can I ask
    you questions today?" If you receive permission, ask about your
    purpose: "What is my essence?" "What is my blessing?" "What is
    my mission?" Feel free to ask clarifying questions! You can also
    ask questions about issues and decisions in your life.

4. If you can, write or record your questions and the answers as you
    go. If this is too distracting, record them immediately after you
    finish.

5. Whether anyone answered or not, say, "Thank you." Do this even
    if you don't like the answers you received. You need to build a
    relationship if you want to return again for more information.

If you haven't already done so, immediately record the questions
you asked and any answers you received, as best you can remember
them. Strive to be exact; watch for the tendency to edit, paraphrase,
or revise. If you received any form of response to your questions, go
on to Chapter 8: Interpreting Your Results to interpret it. If not, try
another self-study method.

Examples

Christine Lennard was working with a coach I trained, Caroll
Schwartz. Under Caroll's guidance, Christine prayed to find her purpose.
Christine is a devout Christian, and prayer is not new for her. She had
experienced connecting with God through prayer previously, but had

never found her purpose. Here is how Christine was experiencing life and what happened when she prayed to learn about her purpose:

"Everything in my life seemed to be a struggling mass of frustration...my marriage, my network marketing business, my relationship with my kids. I was depressed. I was also struggling with God because until recently most of my prayers were answered by Him. I was at my breaking point. He wasn't listening to me.... I guess it was time for me to start listening to Him. Here is the first session I had with Him in prayer about my purpose.

Christine:	Father God in heaven, what is my life's purpose?
God:	*To go make fishers of men.*
Christine:	How?
God:	*Be in relationship.*
Christine:	People I know?
God:	*Yes and no.*
Christine:	How? Pray?
God:	*I will tell you.*
Christine:	How will I make a living?
God:	*I will bless you.*
Christine:	Will I live with Eric (my husband)?
God:	*No.*
Christine:	I am afraid!
God:	*I know.*
Christine:	People I don't know? Where are they?
God:	*Gaylord.*
Christine:	But it doesn't line up with what I know.

God:	*I will tell you what your purpose is.*
Christine:	*When?*
God:	*Soon.*
Christine:	*Sigh...*
God:	*That's as good as it gets!*

"I was overwhelmed at that moment with the confident sense that I am a prayer warrior. This gives me boldness in my prayers with people. I have more authority than I realized. It's not ME doing it—it's God coming through me. I love God. Since this occurred, I have divorced my husband, Eric. (We were already separated, but I resisted divorcing him.) I now teach inmates in the Gaylord County Jail. I also teach at Charlevoix County Jail and have private clients I work with as well. Here is what happened when I prayed for more information:

Christine:	*Please Lord, I am asking you to be very clear about my purpose. I know I can be my purpose in everything I do. Christ Jesus, you died for me, for my sins, my inequity. You already know my history. You've placed in me the desires of my soul and I am totally ready, totally scared, and willing to hear directly from you regarding my purpose...*
God:	*You will love them... Family... They already fit in... You will see broken people. Your prayers will help fill in the gaps.*
Christine:	*I want You to have the glory.*
God:	*You will help them divorce.*
Christine:	*Oh no, I won't!*
God:	*You lived it. You will help them with their purpose.*

Christine:	I will direct them to my coach, Caroll. I need more information, more confidence, before I'm ready to help people.
God:	*You are a prayer warrior. You will not be effective helping others if you are still with Eric. Pray for My people. Stand in the Gap. Listen to My leading. Almost all of the people you talk to and see, you are to pray for.*
Christine:	Father, Thou art awesome... I am probably making this all up.
God!	*DON'T DOUBT ME, CHRISTINE!*

"I was resistant to the idea that I would help people get divorced; it felt wrong somehow. Since then, I have been sought out by ten women to help them in their relationships. I get goose bumps every time I get a call from one."

From these two sessions, Christine came up with the purpose statement, "I am a prayer warrior." There are two reactions she had that are quite common: First, she immediately felt inadequate to do what was being asked of her. Notice that rather than intending to help the people God would send her, she wanted to refer them to her coach because she didn't feel ready. Also, the concern she expressed at the end that she is "making this all up" is very common. People's inner Skeptic can get very wound up about talking to a trusted source. A feeling that it is not real is quite normal, whether the process is working or not. In subsequent sessions, she learned more details about how her purpose works.

Prayer can also work for people who are not devoutly religious. Direct, two-way communication with a trusted source is not reserved for those who have prayed for years. Bill attended the Know Your Purpose Workshop, where a group of coaches and I took all of the participants through the True Purpose process. Not being a very religious man, Bill had never tried to carry on a conversation with God in prayer. Here's what Bill had to say about his experience:

"I prayed before the session started in the morning. I prayed to what I call God, for me a term of convenience. I developed a relationship with God from the 'higher power' approach of 12-step programs (Overeater's Anonymous and Al-Anon). For me, God means the source or spirit of divinity that flows through everything, is within each of us, and connects me to everyone and everything, and everyone and everything to me.

"I began with a few minutes of meditation to clear my mind. Then I prayed, asking God to become available to me. And then I started asking questions. I remember feeling surprised that I got answers and that they didn't feel like they were coming from me. Here is what I wrote in my journal from that interaction:

Bill: Are you there?

God: I'm always here.

Bill: May I ask You questions?

God: Yes, if you can hear the answers.

Bill: What's my purpose in life?

God: Ease their pain.

Bill: What about my pain?

God: It will go.

Bill: How do I ease their pain?

God: Show them the light.

Bill: How do I show them the light?

God: Be the light.

Bill:	What about my wife?
God:	*Ease her pain.*
Bill:	How?
God:	*Compassion. Rise above. Don't come down.*
Bill:	What about my job?
God:	*Let it go.*
Bill:	Thank You.

"I stopped because I felt full—almost overwhelmed by both the experience and what I had learned—and did not feel ready for any more information. I remain amazed by how clear the voice was. I say voice, but I don't remember a sound, just experiencing or knowing the answers so clearly—almost like they appeared on paper without me writing. It did not feel like it was coming from within me. It felt like it was just there, inside me, outside me, just like my sense of the underlying continuity of the universe."

Unlike for Christine, receiving direct answers from God was a new experience for Bill. Like many people, Bill found having direct contact with a trusted source and receiving purpose information overwhelming. This can be a deep, emotional experience. Here's what we know so far about Bill's purpose, based on this interaction:

Essence:	*Be the light*
Blessing:	*Ease people's pain*

Because "Be the light" is about being, not doing, it goes in the essence category. Easing people's pain is an activity, so it is his blessing. We even know one of the steps of his blessing: showing people the light. There are probably more steps and more details to this process, but this is a lot of progress for a first interaction.

Method 4: Meditation

Meditation refers broadly to any of various techniques and practices for focusing and maintaining attention. Different forms of meditation focus attention on different things, such as breathing, an image, or a word or phrase, and are intended to achieve or develop different things. There are both Eastern and Western meditation traditions, although the Eastern forms are more numerous and well known. Meditation can have positive impacts on mood and state of mind, such as reducing stress and creating a sense of calm and well-being, as well as beneficial physiological side effects, such as reducing pulse rate, blood pressure, and heart disease.

While highly beneficial for other things, most forms of meditation are not suitable for finding your life's purpose. The particular form of meditation that works best for finding your purpose is something called a "guided visualization." In this form of meditation, meditators close their eyes and picture a series of events and images (visually) in their mind. This allows the ego to engage in a state where it is capable of contacting and conversing with aspects of the unconscious. This method has the added benefit of providing a means for dealing with ego protectors, something that only a few of the self-study methods provide.

Because of the difficulty of creating and maintaining images in your mind, it may not be easy for you to use this method unless you have a history of meditation. For this reason, beginners may want to use Method 8: Guided Meditation, in which a facilitator guides you through a series of images. Or you may use my audio CD "Know Your Purpose Through Meditation" (available at knowyourpurpose.com/store and Amazon.com).

Some people are not visual by nature and do not experience mental images. For these people, this method is nearly impossible to use. I'm not talking about people who are not predominantly visual; I'm talking about people who never have mental images, even when they dream at night.

While most religious and spiritual traditions include some form of meditation in their history, there are certain denominations that consider meditation to be against their beliefs. As always, I encourage you to look to your own religious and spiritual beliefs to determine whether this method is right for you.

If you have experience with meditation, give this method a try. If you are unable to maintain the images sufficiently to make contact with your trusted source, you can try other self-study methods or get the audio CD "Know Your Purpose Through Meditation."

Exercise: Meditation

This exercise gives a series of steps you can employ to find your purpose. It may require several attempts before you're able to stabilize the images enough to conduct the entire meditation. You may need to spend a considerable amount of time negotiating with your inner protectors before you're able to make contact with your trusted source and learn your purpose.

1. Create quiet, private space and time for yourself. It is best to do this at a time when you are not concerned with pressing deadlines or other distractions. Have a journal and pen handy. Review these instructions carefully before you begin to meditate. You will need to keep your eyes closed, so you'll have to remember the steps!

2. Sit in your favorite meditation posture. If you are unfamiliar with meditation, you can sit comfortably in a chair, with your spine straight and your back supported. Close your eyes and take a few deep breaths.

3. Imagine yourself in a safe place in nature. Don't worry about what image comes; just accept wherever you find yourself. Take a minute to admire the scenery.

4. Invite any parts of you that don't want you to find your purpose
    to show up. They may appear as people, animals, or strange im-
    ages. Don't worry about what form they take.

5. Thank them for coming. Have a conversation with them about
    their concerns. You can negotiate agreements with your parts if
    you need to. Don't make any agreements you won't keep! If no
    parts came, or if they gave you permission, thank your parts and
    proceed. If they didn't give you permission, thank them and STOP
    THE MEDITATION.

6. Ask for your trusted source to come. It may have a familiar ap-
    pearance, an unfamiliar appearance, or no shape or form at all.
    Don't be concerned about how it looks.

7. Check for permission: "Can I ask you questions today?" If you
    hear no response, practice patience. It can sometimes take a
    while to hear answers. Answers may come as words, images,
    memories, feelings, or direct knowing.

8. If you receive permission, ask about your purpose: "What is my
    essence?" "What is my blessing?" "What is my mission?" Feel
    free to ask clarifying questions! You can also ask questions about
    issues and decisions in your life.

9. Whether your trusted source showed up or not, whether it
    answered your questions or not, say, "Thank you." Do this even
    if you don't like the answers you received. You need to build a
    relationship if you want to return again for more information.

10. When you feel complete, slowly open your eyes and begin to
    move. Immediately record the questions you asked and any
    answers you received, as best you can remember them. Strive to
    be exact; watch for the tendency to edit, paraphrase, or revise.
    Also record any agreements you made with your parts. If you

don't keep these agreements, you can expect to have trouble connecting to your trusted source later.

If you received any form of response to your questions, go on to Chapter 8: Interpreting Your Results to interpret it. If not, try another self-study method.

Example

Bob, an early client of mine, hired me to help him find his life's purpose. I talked with Bob to discover what trusted sources exist in his universe. Bob is a Buddhist and, like many Buddhists, he meditates regularly. I discovered that in his meditation practice he visits a statue of Buddha and they have conversations (visualized in his mind, not a physical statue). Not only did Bob have a meditation practice, but he was already having direct interactions with his trusted source! I set Bob up with specific questions to ask this Buddha statue as homework. Here is what happened when Bob meditated next:

"My method is to sit on the couch in my downstairs office where my Buddha thangka (a traditional sacred image) hangs above and be-hind me, lower the lights, play some meditation music (in this case, Tibetan Buddhist music and chants) and relax with my eyes closed. I breathe deeply and clear my mind for as long as that takes, and once I feel relaxed and present, I visualize myself strolling down the beach alongside a spectacular blue ocean early in the morning. From there, I guide myself through a practiced visualization that takes me into conversation with the Self inside me, the essence of my soul.

"In this visualization I found that the weather was perfect, warm and clear, and I was feeling especially good as I strolled along the edge of the water. I walked to the usual waterfall spot and stripped off my clothes, let the warm, sparkling water pour over me, and allowed myself to shed my identity and become a temple monk who can enter the inner sanctum of my temple to sit face-to-face with Lord Buddha. Through a silent prayer I called my temple into being, and it slowly came into view before me, a medium-sized Asian pagoda made of wood and stone.

"After asking for permission to enter, and hearing the temple Priestess's traditional welcome, 'Yes... you are *always* welcome here,' I walked through the front door and down the long stone hallway to the cave-like underground area, where I found candles and incense already lit in preparation for my arrival. Buddha gave me every indication that he was expecting me by saying, as soon as I had seated myself, 'So, you are here to speak to me about your purpose.'

"I told him yes, that I had come for his guidance and counsel on what my purpose is and how I could best go about manifesting it in the world. He said, 'I think you already know your purpose, and that, in fact, you have known it for many years. It is as you suspected: You are a force for Peace. You have resisted and questioned this purpose because of the pain you feel at having exerted so little conscious effort to make this purpose a reality in your life, but this experience of pain is based on your assumption that you have not been moving toward the perfect manifestation of your purpose all of your life. This painful sensation also wrongly assumes that you have not been a force for Peace since the very moment you were born, and that you have wasted time by not putting your purpose into greater action.'

"He went on to say many other things, including that my blessing is to be a Guardian of the Temple in the outer world, helping to usher other people across the threshold while preventing the entrance of energies that do not serve; that I can manifest my purpose through merely breathing, as well as radiate it during the process of any activity I do all day long, such as my web development work, parenting, or driving my car; that my ego wrongly believes my purpose must take a certain pre-determined form and finding out what that form is will enable me to

actually be 'doing my purpose'; and that the best way to have an experience of manifesting my purpose would be for me to do it by engaging in
an activity for which I have a natural aptitude and for which I feel joy,
enthusiasm, and passion. Through some back and forth, we determined
together that music, filmmaking, and writing were all activities at which
I had natural skill and for which I felt great enthusiasm, and that I
(particularly, my ego) would be likely to feel most like I was really 'doing'
my purpose well if I chose to manifest it through one of those avenues.
One other important point he told me was that my financial success was
virtually guaranteed if I chose any of those avenues, as he pointed out
that I had been involved in writing and music in some form or another
all my life, both for fun and for money.

"When I had asked all of the questions I could think of, and he
had finished offering me his perspective on my purpose, I bowed and
thanked him as graciously as I knew how. As always, I asked for permission to leave the temple, and heard the disembodied voice of the
Priestess say once again, 'You are *always* welcome here.' At that, I made
the journey back above ground and out through the temple doors. Once
I had walked several paces across the sand, I turned to the temple once
again, raised my hands as before, and prayed for the temple and my
garments to fade away once again into non-time and non-space. As
usual, my original clothing was waiting for me right where I had left it,
and I took a little time to ponder what this confirmation of my purpose
might mean for my life as I dressed and began strolling back down the
beach toward home."

Since Bob already had a relationship with his trusted source via
meditation, it was very simple and easy for him to go and ask it questions about his purpose. If you do not have experience leading yourself
through guided visualizations, it may be much more difficult for you than
it was for Bob. In this case, guided meditation may be a better approach,
or you can try other self-study methods.

Method 5: Journaling

Many people keep a journal, a place where they write down their thoughts and feelings. There are many types of journaling, including automatic writing and non-dominant hand writing. While all of these approaches have great value, the particular type of journaling we will employ is called "active imagination."

This is the same method we used to negotiate with your parts to get permission to find your purpose. In this case, instead of dialoguing with one of your parts, you will be dialoguing with your trusted source. It is highly effective for this use; typically over 75% of people make contact on the first try. As before, you will write both sides of the dialogue, either by hand or on a computer.

This is the method I prefer to use on a daily basis. For many people, it is the most convenient one over the long term to have an ongoing dialogue with their trusted source. For example, it is quicker and more convenient than Method 4: Meditation or Method 6: Dreaming and provides a handy written record. Unlike dreaming, meditation, and prayer, you don't have to remember what happened and write it down afterwards. You write it down as you go.

This method works well with internal, personal, and universal trusted sources. It also has the added advantage of working for people of any psychological, spiritual, or religious belief system. In some faiths it is not permitted to write the full name of God (for example, it is forbidden under Jewish law). If this is true for you and you plan to communicate with a deity whose name you cannot write, use an abbreviation or symbol that is a permissible representation. Where such restrictions exist, there are usually acceptable substitutes.

There are two common experiences people have with respect to the speed of the process. Some people write down the question, then pause and wait, and then write down the response. The process takes on a sedate, reflective pace. Others find that the interaction is occurring very rapidly in their head and their writing can barely keep up. The process becomes almost frantic! Both styles of active imagination are entirely legitimate; neither way is better, and neither is more accurate. People don't seem to have any choice about which way it happens, so whichever way it happens for you, I suggest you just go with it.

There is an interesting downside to this method: It is so very simple, people have trouble believing that it is working. When people are conversing with their trusted source in active imagination, they often hear a running skeptical soundtrack in their head at the same time: "This is too simple; it can't be this easy. How do I know that this is really my soul talking? I must be making it all up." It's best not to worry about whether it's working or not while you're doing it. We will explore how to distinguish a legitimate communication from a trusted source in Chapter 8: Interpreting Your Results.

If these skeptical thoughts become too strong to allow you to focus, you need to stop having an interaction with your trusted source and start having a conversation with your inner Skeptic! See what your Skeptic needs in order to allow you to do the process without too much interference. You can figure out later whether you made it all up or not.

Resistance from the ego can show up in another form as well: forgetting to write down both sides of the conversation. Often clients will just write a running commentary, rather than naming the participants in a two-way conversation.

Exercise: Active Imagination

This time, rather than talking to your ego parts to get permission to find your purpose, you'll be communicating directly with a trusted source. Just write out both sides of the conversation, putting your name in front of your questions and the trusted source's name in front of the responses. Here are the steps:

1. Create quiet, private space and time for yourself. It is best to do this at a time when you are not concerned with pressing deadlines or other distractions. Bring a journal and a pen (or a computer, if you are more comfortable typing). Sit and relax for a few minutes to focus yourself in present time.

2. Ask for permission: Write your name, followed by a request to talk to your trusted source. "Steve: Soul, is it okay if I ask you questions about my purpose today?"

3. Write down the name of your trusted source, and then write the answer to the question. Don't spend time thinking about it; just write.

4. Write your name followed by a question in your journal: "What is my essence?" "What is my blessing?" or "What is my mission?" You may ask any question you like.

5. Write the trusted source's name followed by a response. The answer may be a feeling, image, memory, or actual words. Don't worry about whether you are "making it up" or not.

6. When you are done (or when the trusted source indicates that it is done), end by thanking it. Thank it even if you have received no responses whatsoever! Thank it even if you didn't like the information the trusted source gave you or it withheld something you wanted desperately to know! Thank it even if you don't believe it was really your trusted source!

When you write your journal entries, be sure to write your name in front of your questions. Write a suitable name for your trusted source in front of the answers. If you don't do this, you are journaling, but you are not having a two-way conversation with your trusted source. If you got specific responses to your questions, go to Chapter 8: Interpreting Your Results to evaluate them. Do this even if you're not sure whether it was really your trusted source; we'll work on whether it was real or not.

Example

Jeffrey Van Dyk is another leader in the Purposeful Coach Community. He supervises the coaching staff in the Know Your Purpose Teleseminar and the Purposeful Coach Training, among other things. Michael "Coop" Cooper is a client of his; he first made contact with his trusted source via active imagination. Here is what occurred. Note that he did not give his trusted source a specific name, but instead chose to call it simply "Trusted Source":

Michael:	Trusted Source?
Trusted Source:	Yes, we are here.
Michael:	May I know my purpose now?
Trusted Source:	You have done well. Yes, you may know your purpose.
Michael:	Thank you! What is my purpose?
Trusted Source:	Your purpose is to illuminate the world.
Michael:	Wow, that is a tall order! Can you please clarify what that means?
Trusted Source:	Yes. Your purpose is to help each person that you meet to bring as much of their gifts and talents, which are light, to the world as possible.
Michael:	May I know my essence?
Trusted Source:	Yes. Your essence is being a light. You are energy, or light. You are an example. You must tell people what your gift is and show them by helping them bring their gifts to the world.
Michael:	Will I be able to earn a living by doing this?
Trusted Source:	The more you live your gift, the greater your rewards.
Michael:	May I know my blessing?

Trusted Source: *Yes. Your blessing is to help people who want to be inspirations for others to bring their true gifts to the world.*

Michael: What state are my clients in when they need my blessing?

Trusted Source: *They feel alone, frustrated, and want to learn how to scale their impact.*

Michael: What are the steps of my blessing? What is the process?

Trusted Source: *1. You will help people identify their gifts and talents— the things they are uniquely designed to do and are the best at.*

2. You will help them eliminate as much distraction and other tasks as possible so that they can give the most benefit to the world.

3. You will help them hone their gifts and talents for greater impact.

4. You will help them develop skills to support their gifts and talents, such as drawing clear boundaries, setting clear expectations, discovering their own blocks, and conquering the fear that comes with changing the world.

5. You will help them become self-sustaining and quit when they tell you they no longer need your help.

Michael: Is that it?

Trusted Source: *Yes. It's that simple.*

Michael: What is the effect or impact on others when they receive my blessing? How are they changed?

Trusted Source:	*They are lit up, expanded, self-sustaining, and making an impact on a large scale. They are literally changing the world. They are happy and fulfilled. Their lives are enriched and they enrich the lives of thousands.*
Michael:	In what state are they when the process is complete?
Trusted Source:	*They are self-sustainable. They have everything they need to make their impact on the world.*
Michael:	How will I know they are self-sustainable?
Trusted Source:	*They will tell you they no longer need your help.*
Michael:	What do I need to do to develop my gift?
Trusted Source:	*Nothing. You already have everything you need to live your gift. You have worked hard and learned much over your lifetime to prepare you for this. It is all in place now. Go fearlessly and give yourself in service. The world will be a better place when you leave it.*
Michael:	For whom is my blessing intended?
Trusted Source:	*Your blessing is for people who are making a difference in the world or feel called to make a difference. You are to work with any person who calls you and expresses the need for your help because they want to make a difference in the world. If they do not say that specifically, you may choose not to work with them.*
Michael:	What if it goes against my belief systems or they want to do damage?
Trusted Source:	*The people who want to make a difference in the world are all trying to improve the planet. Some will*

succeed and some will fail. There is no good or bad or damage. There is only an impact.

Michael: What is my mission?

Trusted Source: *Your mission is to help luminaries, leaders, newsmakers, and society shapers to be examples for others by bringing their gifts to inspire humanity to evolve to a more sustainable way of living.*

Michael: Wow! What do you mean by "sustainable way of living"?

Trusted Source: *Inspiration helps people acknowledge the importance of life and things only human beings are capable of experiencing and creating. Humanity's future is in peril because too many people are unconsciously living and destroying the future possibilities of life as you know it.*

Michael: Am I supposed to do this alone?

Trusted Source: *No. There are thousands of people doing what you do in their own unique way. Your job is to find your own truth and live it in your own style. Why do you think you were born on a farm and turned out to be gay? That was by design. Farming represents humility and understanding patterns; gay represents breaking the rules imposed by society. Your education allows you to relate to any person in any sphere of the world.*

Michael: In what way am I to change the world?

Trusted Source: *You enable others to change the world. By doing so, you have a very broad and meaningful impact on the world. You have a responsibility to meet and you are more than capable of meeting it.*

Michael: Am I a messenger? If so, what is my message?

Trusted Source: *Yes. Anyone can change the world. Everyone has a responsibility to hone their gifts and become fully expressed. By doing so, they open up the possibility of changing the world. People who have a desire to inspire others build a platform to give direction and share their own messages.*

Michael: Before, you said I should work with luminaries, leaders, newsmakers, and society shapers. Can you please be more specific?

Trusted Source: *Why do you want a direct answer here? Are you afraid?*

Michael: Yes. I'm afraid that I don't know what to do or how to make a living doing this.

Trusted Source: *We told you that you would always have enough abundance to sustain you and that you will prosper beyond your wildest dreams.*

Michael: I'm just struggling financially now and this situation is causing me lots of anxiety, so I'm asking for as much help as you can give me to get through this situation and live my purpose.

Trusted Source: *We understand. You are to take the next ten days and write what you know about gifts. We will give you all the information you need to make this a very successful venture. Clear your calendar and write. You will be fine.*

Michael: Is that in the form of a website or book or article?

Trusted Source: *It does not matter. Just give away what you know. You will always have more than enough abundance to sustain you.*

Michael:	How will I find clients?
Trusted Source:	*They will find you.*
Michael:	What do I do with my current business?
Trusted Source:	*Apply your gifts to it or whatever business you want. Support your current partners by helping them develop their gifts. You will all prosper beyond your wildest dreams.*
Michael:	What do I do about my current financial situation?
Trusted Source:	*Ask for help. Get out of your own way. Lead your company to produce more than enough money for you and your partners by simplifying what you know.*
Michael:	Am I supposed to be out selling?
Trusted Source:	*No. Your job is to provide leadership and counsel. Selling would take you away from your mission. Write a vision statement for the business that contains 13 words. Strip away everything that does not directly connect to that vision statement.*
Michael:	Can you help me write the vision statement?
Trusted Source:	*Yes. "Create opportunities and processes for people to bring their best into the world."*
Michael:	What if my partners don't agree with this?
Trusted Source:	*They will. It is truth and what you have always been attempting to clarify.*
Michael:	I'm overwhelmed and afraid of the magnitude of my purpose and mission.
Trusted Source:	*You are God. You have the power and the skill to inspire the world to change. Give yourself permission to live your gift. Fear is a sign that*

> *you need to develop courage, which is required to experience all gifts fully.*
>
> Michael: How do I develop courage? I thought I had everything to live my mission.
>
> Trusted Source: *You have the courage, but you have not given yourself permission to use it, to hone it, to strengthen it in this endeavor. All it takes is a simple decision.*
>
> Michael: Thank you.
>
> Trusted Source: *You are welcome. We love you.*

A tremendous amount of information has been revealed here! The sweeping, confident nature of the trusted source's responses is common when a genuine connection has been achieved. Michael's concerns and feeling of overwhelm are quite normal, too!

Michael is using many of the specific questions for clarifying a blessing and a mission from the section "Asking Good Questions" in Chapter 5: Direct Access to Purpose. His first question, though, is "What is my purpose?" The answers to this and the following question illustrate the pitfalls of asking the question this way.

"Illuminate the world" is mission information. It is a single task that can only be done once, and it is truly grand in scope. "Help each person... bring as much of their gifts and talents... to the world as possible" is a blessing, something you can do over and over again with different people. Because the question "What is my purpose?" is so vague and broad, you can receive different types of information in response. This can be confusing, which is why it is usually best to ask three questions instead: "What is my essence?" "What is my blessing?" "What is my mission?"

Michael's subsequent questions sorted everything out, so it wasn't a problem in the end. We will talk in much more detail in Chapter 8: Interpreting Your Results about how to distinguish what kinds of information you have received.

Even if this method doesn't work for you, come back and try it again after you've gotten another method to work. It will often start working once you have made contact with your trusted source some other way.

Method 6: Dreaming

I've placed this method last among the self-study methods, because it is the least convenient to use and can yield the most complicated and confusing results. The interpretation of dreams is a discipline that requires years to truly master. Even if you're training in working with dreams, the interpretation of your own dreams is a chancy process, because the interpretation is being performed by the ego, which is a highly subjective observer. As a self-study method, using dreaming to find your life's purpose essentially depends on getting lucky. "Getting lucky" means that you have a simple dream that clearly and specifically illustrates or articulates your life purpose.

Sleeping dreams are the most direct access possible to the unconscious. Therefore, dreams give you the most accurate representation and rendering of what's occurring in your unconscious. Unfortunately, dreams can reveal any of the contents of the unconscious, not just your purpose. Using dreaming as a method for finding your purpose entails trying to influence the dreaming process to access purpose content in the unconscious, as opposed to all of the other things the unconscious contains.

You can influence your dreams by making a specific request of your unconscious on a given night to offer up information about your purpose. This is effectively a roll of the dice; it either works or it doesn't. If there are other pressing issues going on in your life, your dreams will probably reflect them, rather than your purpose.

This method works for anyone who has dreams and can remember them. It is critical when using dreaming to record your dreams immediately upon waking. Not only do most people forget their dreams in the first few minutes after they awaken, but the ego starts to edit the details of them as well. For this reason, it is important to prepare, before you go to sleep, to record your dream upon awakening.

Another disadvantage of this method is its inefficiency. As a dialogue, it takes a long time, because you can only effectively ask one question per night. Most of the other direct access methods set up a two-way dialogue that occurs in real time. This is a far better way of communicating information. Nevertheless, I have known several people, myself included, who first made contact with their purpose via dreaming. If the dream you receive is not clear and explicit about your purpose, you have two choices:

1. You can disregard it and go on to use other methods.

2. You can use the dream work method (Method 10 in Chapter 7: Facilitated Methods). This involves finding and engaging the services of someone who is properly trained in dream work and dream interpretation.

Exercise: Dreaming

Since dreams process a lot of unconscious material, it works best to do this exercise at a time when you're not faced with great stress in your life. If there are work or family problems or major decisions that you're facing, your dreams may tend to focus there rather than on your purpose. It also works to choose a night when you have plenty of uninterrupted time for sleeping, as well as time available in the morning to record whatever dreams you have. Do not drink alcohol or take drugs before sleeping, as this can interfere with the dreaming process.

Before going to bed, place a means of recording your dreams nearby. This could be a journal and pen, a tape recorder or digital voice recorder, or a computer. Make sure that you have enough time between when you awaken and when you have to start work or other activities to record your dream. Fully recording a dream can sometimes take half an hour or even more.

Once you're in bed and starting to relax, but before you fall asleep, it is important to set an intention for your dreaming. This maximizes the chances that you will have a dream about your purpose. Go ahead, fall asleep and see what happens.

1. Choose a night when you will have time after you awaken. It will work best if you are not consumed with concern about other issues in your life. Put either a tape recorder or a journal, pen, and flashlight by your bed. This will allow you to record your dream immediately when you wake up.

2. Right before going to bed, ask for a dream that will make your life's purpose clear to you. Set the following intentions:

    a. That you will have a dream about your life's purpose

    b. That it will be clear, simple, and easy to understand

    c. That you will remember it when you awaken

3. When you awaken, immediately record as much of your dream as you can. Do this even if you wake in the middle of the night. Record everything, whether it makes sense to you or not. Include anything you felt or knew in the dream, not just what happened. RECORD ANY DREAM YOU HAVE, NO MATTER HOW SMALL OR IRRELEVANT IT SEEMS.

4. In addition to what occurred in the dream, you may have certain feelings, senses, memories, or realizations upon awakening. Record these as well.

You may have a dream that is confusing to you. What we're looking for here is a dream in which your purpose is clearly written or spoken; this way it will not be a challenge for you to interpret it. Typically 10%

of people or fewer have such a clear dream on the first try. If you do not have a simple, clear dream where the message about your purpose is obvious, you have three choices:

1. You can try again another night.

2. You can find someone trained in the interpretation of dreams and use Method 10: Dream Work. See the resources in the Appendix for information on finding people trained in dream work.

3. You can try another method.

Example

Unless you are trained in the interpretation of dreams, we will need to get a very simple, clear dream in order for this method to work. Here are two examples of the kind of dream I'm talking about:

"I set the intentions according to the exercise and fell asleep. In my dream, God appeared to me. He looked at me, then handed me an envelope. I knew that the envelope contained my purpose. I opened the envelope, took out the paper inside, and read it."

This dream came to a coach during the Purposeful Coach Training, while she was learning to find her clients' purposes. Unfortunately, she didn't write down the contents of the envelope when she awoke and quickly forgot what it said. This brings up an important aspect of this method: While you are asleep, your ego has a very difficult time controlling what is happening in the dream. Therefore, when your ego tries to resist finding your purpose via the dreaming method, it usually does so by preventing you from writing down the dream immediately when you awaken. You may find yourself having thoughts like, "This dream can't be about my purpose." "This dream doesn't count. I wish I'd had a real dream!" This is the sound of the ego dismissing the message from the unconscious. Don't let this happen to you! WRITE YOUR DREAM DOWN IMMEDIATELY, WHETHER YOU LIKE IT OR UNDERSTAND IT OR NOT! Worry about interpreting it later.

Here's another example:

"There was complete blackness, no images at all. A booming voice said, 'Your purpose is to help others find their path.' The dream ended and I woke up."

This was a dream I had years ago. It was how I first learned my purpose! It is the only dream I've ever had where there were no visual images whatsoever.

Notice the common elements between these two dreams:

- ✓ They are unambiguous and easy to interpret.
- ✓ They are obviously about life purpose.
- ✓ The purpose is communicated clearly, in words (spoken or written).

This is the kind of dream we're looking for: simple, easy, direct, and explicit. If this is what you got, congratulations! Skip down to Chapter 8: Interpreting Your Results. If not, keep using this method or try another one.

Chapter Seven

Facilitated Methods

Many people will require qualified assistance to establish a clear connection to their soul. If you have tried all of the self-study methods and have not been receiving answers, facilitated methods are probably the way to go. Often the issue is ego blocks that are too difficult to clear by yourself.

In the self-study methods, you are asking questions of your trusted source. In facilitated methods, the facilitator is usually asking questions of your trusted source. Unlike a session with a psychic or channeler, the answers come through you, rather than through them. It is the facilitator's responsibility to create conditions in which you can receive (and speak) answers directly from your trusted source. This can be a powerful and moving experience!

In some cases, there is an exact correspondence between a self-study method and a facilitated method. You are doing essentially the same thing, but this time you are doing it with trained help. Meditation and dream work each have both a self-study and a facilitated version, and Voice Dialogue can be viewed as a facilitated version of the active imagination exercise. Read about all of them and see which one draws you the most. You can learn more about each method by referring to the sources listed in the resources in the Appendix.

One big disadvantage of facilitated methods is cost. People who have spent time and money getting trained in these methodologies usually charge for their services. It is up to you to decide how much knowing your purpose is worth to you and how much you can afford to pay in order to know. It is also your responsibility to check the training and qualifications of the practitioner.

Don't assume that someone trained in Voice Dialogue or hypnotherapy is also trained in finding your purpose. Each of these is a general methodology that can be used for many things. Practitioners are often trained to use these methods for counseling and therapy rather than for finding life's purpose. Also, don't assume that someone who does life purpose work is familiar with the concepts in this book. Most "life purpose coaches" are only trained in indirect methods for finding purpose.

Method 7: Voice Dialogue

Voice Dialogue is a system for exploring the psyche developed by Hal and Sidra Stone. This is my favorite method by far and the one I employ in my one-on-one client work. Voice Dialogue deals directly with the aspects of the psyche by literally providing each sub-personality, or "voice," its own seat. The Voice Dialogue facilitator walks you through some simple steps to gain access to different parts of your psyche. Although this method is extremely simple and easily understood, it should only be attempted by those who have received the proper training. Delving into other people's psyches is not a casual exercise for beginners.

There are a number of other methods that I'm lumping together under this category. They include Internal Family Systems therapy (IFS), gestalt therapy, and the "parts work" aspect of neuro-linguistic programming (NLP). Although the techniques vary somewhat, they are all effectively doing the same thing: carrying on direct conversations with specific parts of the client's psyche. Although I will use the term "Voice Dialogue" throughout this chapter, I am really writing about all of these methods.

Voice Dialogue is by far the best method for clearing ego blocks. This is because it allows the facilitator to address and deal with the individual parts of your psyche that have concerns or issues about you learning your purpose. It is also effective for establishing a direct line of communication to a trusted source and asking specific questions about your purpose.

The way the method works is this. The client starts out sitting in a chair. Let's say the client's name is Mary. The facilitator wants to talk to Mary's Protector. Mary gets up and sits or stands somewhere else. This new spot is now the spot for the Protector. The facilitator doesn't address her as Mary in her new location, but as "Protector." For example, "So, Protector, how do you protect Mary?" Although Mary may not feel any differently from when she started, her job is to respond as if she were the Protector; for example, "I protect Mary by making sure she doesn't walk in front of moving buses." Although some people may find it awkward to talk about themselves in the third person, it is a habit that most people pick up quickly. This greatly enhances the process of allowing the individual parts of the psyche to speak for themselves.

When the facilitator wants to talk to a different part of the client's psyche, say the inner Critic, he asks Mary to move to a new spot. This new spot is the Critic's spot. The facilitator might ask, "So, Critic, what kinds of things do you criticize Mary about?" Mary answers as the Critic, "Where do I start? There are so many things wrong with her…"

What is surprising about Voice Dialogue and similar methods is how simple they are and how well they work. Clients are usually surprised at how easily they can access their parts and at the interesting and revealing things the parts have to say.

All of this is pretty standard psychological exploration, and it works incredibly well for clearing ego blocks. But none of it will find your purpose! In order to find your purpose, Voice Dialogue can be used as a direct access method to communicate with a trusted source. Continuing the above example, the facilitator wants to find Mary's purpose, so he asks her to move to a new spot, this time a spot for Mary's soul. Mary moves to a new spot. The facilitator asks, "So, Soul, what is Mary's essence?" Mary answers as her soul, "I'm glad you asked. I've been wanting her to find out about her purpose for some time now..."

Like active imagination, the access is so simple and so direct that people may have difficulty believing that it's really working. I have found Voice Dialogue to work about 60% of the time for establishing a connection to a trusted source.

Example

Jessica was another of Caroll Schwartz's purpose clients. Caroll and I agreed that Voice Dialogue was necessary for dealing with some of the blocks in her ego. With Caroll watching, Jessica and I did a session lasting several hours, dealing with the concerns that her Controller, Critic, Skeptic, and several other parts had about finding her purpose. Jessica had been struggling internally with these parts, trying to get them to stop controlling, criticizing, doubting, etc. Jessica moved to different seats in the room, each time taking on the persona of one of the individual parts. All eventually agreed that it was in her best interests (and theirs) to find her purpose. (You can find descriptions of these different parts in the section "Understanding Inner Protectors" in Chapter 4: Clearing a Path through the Ego.)

Since we were already engaged in a Voice Dialogue process, we decided to try to connect with Jessica's preferred trusted source, God, using the same method. Jessica moved to a different seat and began speaking as God, rather than as one of her ego parts. This is the conversation that ensued:

Tim: Welcome.

God: *Thanks.*

Tim: How are we doing here? I'm curious for Your opinion.

God: *You're doing well; you're good at what you do.*

Tim: Thank You. First of all, it would be very useful to hear Your plan for Jessica, Your mission for her, to the extent that it's okay for her to know it now.

God: *First I have to tell her about the role of each part of her.*

Tim: That's great; please do.

God: *Jessica, the Skeptic helps you in determining whether something is a good risk. When I put skepticism in your path, I want you to judge it. I'm putting stops in front of you, to signal that this may not be the best choice for you.*

                The point is that you need to listen. The Skeptic was meant to help you, not to hurt you. I want you to create a different relationship with it. Know that intuition is a guide. Listen to it.

                The Critic is a part that damaged your ego; I'm sorry about that. I do apologize for that, but it's criticizing you to make you a better person so that you can fulfill what you need to fulfill. If you fulfill your purpose, then it won't criticize you as much.

Here's the deal, Jessica. The Controller is not meant to control you; it's meant for Me to be able to get you to do things that I need you to do. You fight it too much. You want the control. You're just getting further and further away from what you're supposed to do by not listening to this part. You're making it harder for the parts to do their job, because you're resisting them more. Don't look at this as something that is controlling you. We mapped it out together before you came down here; you just forgot.

You're prepared to do everything I need you to do. The Controller is just there to make sure you're protected, because you're going to accumulate a fortune from this. That is what all of your training has been for. That's why you handled money: so you would know what to do and you wouldn't get screwed.

Let the Controller do its job and you'll be fine. Don't fight it.

Okay, I'm good.

Tim: I think it's really critical for her to understand that these parts are Your servants in that process. She thinks they're the enemy. You put them in her to perform these functions, and she needs to partner with them in that, rather than resist them.

God: She *needs* to listen to her intuition, because I keep telling her and she keeps ignoring it. She's making everyone's job harder.

Tim: I know that she knows her purpose, but I think it's going to make a difference hearing it come from You.

God: She is supposed to be the conduit for people to realize that no matter what situation they're in, no matter how bad it is, no matter what they've gone through, they can still achieve their dreams.

Jessica is personable and young enough that she can reach all audiences. Her job is to bring people together; she is the access for people to see that it is possible for them to have anything they want, no matter what their circumstances. She's going to break through the barriers of all of the reasons why people can't. She's here to cause a transformation in the world.

There are a lot of unhappy people who think they can't live the life of their dreams. She's here to show them that they can. I've brought her all of the people she needs and everything she needs to do it.

She needs to get over the fact that she's going to be on TV and be successful. She needs to get over it and accept that it is fine.

She can't just tell people that they can live their dreams and then stop. She has to create the business, a place for people to go; otherwise, there won't be any changes. It will be a resource center.

Tim, you're going to be part of the resource center. You're going to help people know what their purpose is. That's why she was supposed to find you, to see whether she liked this process.

Jessica's fear is that she's not going to be able to walk down the street and do her thing, that she's

> *going to be stopped and have to coach people. She*
> *wants to have her life and have this, too.*
>
> *She can have both, because I'm giving her a*
> *place to send people. She's the messenger.*

Tim: When they come to her for coaching, she says, "I don't do that, here's the website and my card."

God: *Exactly. She can get people to do anything. She has to have a pure intention or it won't work, and this is the purest intention in the world.*

> *Do you have a sentence for her yet?*

Tim: A purpose statement, You mean? As a summary?

God: *Yes. How are you doing in this process?*

Tim: If You feel it would serve her for me to boil it down to a sentence, then I absolutely will. Is that what You feel should happen?

God: *Yes.*

Tim: She is to show people that regardless of their circumstances, they can have whatever they want and they can have it now. It's not her job to do that for them; it's her job to connect them to those who can. Is that it?

God: *Yes. I will protect her along the way. The answer is in her; she just thinks it isn't. She can check in with Me all of the time.*

Tim: I imagine that would be very easy for her to do.

God: *She's one of the few people who have a direct link, but she doesn't use it. She keeps buying all of these books and she reads and rereads them, but she doesn't get it. She doesn't need to read it ten times; she has a direct link to Me. She knows. She's having a connection to Me right now.*

Tim: *Caroll can offer her some simple procedures to use, too. Thank You so much for coming.*

God: *Be easy now. This is still kind of... (Jessica squirms and giggles)*

Tim: *Kind of what?*

God: *Her mannerisms are coming out and I don't quite know what to do with it.*

Tim: *I understand. She doesn't quite know how to have God talking through her mouth. It's not something she's used to.*

God: *This is the first time she's ever done it to other people. Wait a minute, that's not true. She does it all of the time; she's just not conscious of it. Jessica's ego is trying to fight this a little.*

Tim: *I can see how this would be a gift necessary to her purpose. When people come to her, if she can just efficiently read them and direct them to the appropriate resource, she makes a much better traffic director. This is what she really is. With a direct connection to You, she has an immediate ability to direct them the right way. Is that correct?*

God: *Yes.*

Tim: *Thank You very much for Your gifts to us. Is there anything else that needs to be said?*

God: *No. Thank you very much.*

Tim: *Jessica, move back over to your seat. It sounds different when it's coming from God, doesn't it?*

Jessica: *Church people say you have to go to church to get that.*

Tim: *God is everywhere.*

Jessica: I know. I just don't know why I don't listen to myself more. Do you have any suggestions for how to do that?

Tim: Treat your parts as trusted advisors. They are your pals. God sent them to help you.

   If you want to find the most efficient, most purposeful, most successful, most fulfilling way to live your life, you'll be listening to your parts. If you were listening, they wouldn't be shouting as loudly. People get loud when they're being ignored. So do parts.

   These parts are going to do all of the work: getting your book published, putting up a website, signing contracts with service providers. All of that legwork has to be done, and they're the only ones who can do it.

   You should be thanking them for being here to help you. Then they'd be much more relaxed. They're all afraid you're going to fire them.

Jessica: I know.

I have used Voice Dialogue over a hundred times to speak to trusted sources. It is a strange and wonderful experience to hear people speaking as their trusted source, directly and simply answering questions that have perplexed them for years. What I found so remarkable about this session, and what had me choose it as the example for this book, was the way in which Jessica's trusted source explicitly told her the proper role of each of her parts. So often people dislike how their parts operate and try to get rid of them, instead of trying to establish a better relationship with them.

Method 8: Guided Meditation

This is effectively the same as Method 4: Meditation, except that in this case, the people seeking their purpose are facilitated through the meditation by someone trained to do so. While there are many forms of meditation, again, it is the guided visualization aspect of meditation that is employed. The facilitator suggests or offers a series of images to the meditators that supports them in making contact with a trusted source. The facilitator may also offer specific questions to help the meditators' ego get as much information as possible from the trusted source. For people not experienced in meditation, a guided meditation is far more effective than trying to learn to do it solo. Again, as with the meditation method, certain religious denominations take a dim view of meditation. As with any method, do not use it if it violates your beliefs or practices.

One significant disadvantage of guided meditation is that there are no specific certifications or qualifications for guided meditation practitioners. This means that it may be difficult to establish whether someone is sufficiently skilled to lead you through a meditative process. It is highly unlikely that any form of meditation could cause you harm, but it is entirely possible that someone without the proper training could waste your time and money.

I have used guided meditation very effectively in my workshops and coach trainings. A significant advantage of it is that I can lead a large group of people through a meditation simultaneously, enabling many people to find their purpose at once.

This method also allows you to carry on conversations and negotiations with ego protectors, thereby increasing the chances of finding your purpose. Not all people who lead meditations understand how to deal effectively with ego protectors! For these reasons, I've created an audio CD, "Know Your Purpose Through Meditation," which hundreds of people have found highly effective for finding their purpose. When this ego negotiation is included in the meditation process, it consistently achieves success rates of 75% or higher.

Example

This woman connected to her trusted source while taking the Purposeful Coach Training and learning to work with clients on their purpose. The images came to her while I was leading the group through a guided meditation.

"I began down a sandy path amid luscious tall green tropical trees, vines, and plants. Flowers hung in places, orchids. Other flowers in red and fuchsia showed here and there. I saw a lake to my right. Then I thought it was too big for a lake; I couldn't see any shore on the other side, so it could have been an ocean. I came to a clearing, a sandy clearing, opening to the water on the right. There was a circle of stones that had been used as a fire ring. I took the firestones and, kissing them one by one, laid them in a circle around me and asked for their protection. Then I waited for a protector.

"Eventually, a black panther came slowly toward me on the path (beyond where I had entered). He paced slowly around the circle clockwise, then counterclockwise. We maintained eye contact, and I thanked him profusely for coming to me. I recognized him to be the panther from Rilke's poem 'The Panther,' finally set free.

"He seemed to know all of the prayers I had said for him, and this protection was in gratitude for my loving him. He went up into the nearest tree, telling me that he would keep constant watch there. The panther and I waited for the messenger bringing some information about my life purpose.

"Eventually, a canoe came gliding up out of the bay. It had five brown women in it. The two youngest jumped out and slid the canoe onto the sand. Then the other two got out also, and then the last, the eldest, was suddenly seated in the midst of all of them in front of me. I asked the youngest, to the far right, her age. She said '18.' The one on the far left said '26.' The one to her right said '44.' The second in from the right said '60.' When I looked at the woman in the center, I already knew her to be Grandmother (archetypally), and then I saw that she was my own Abuelita, my maternal grandmother, who died when I was seven. I began to cry, but she said I shouldn't cry because it wasn't a sad day."

"I asked them what they had to tell me about my purpose, and they said that the important thing to know is not to hold back. 'Think of the Golden Age of Spain that is living in you. Our people need you to tell the story.' Then they said, 'Do not let your mother stop you, or stop the things that are meant to come through you. To let her stop you would be to allow a pea to impede the flow of a great river.' Then they returned to the canoe and were gone. The panther came out of the tree and said good-bye. I asked him if he would come to talk sometime and he said 'yes.'"

"I placed the stones back into the fire circle and left the clearing back down the path I'd come from."

I learned from her later what the "Golden Age of Spain" meant. Throughout much of Spanish history, Muslims, Christians, and Jews coexisted peacefully in a multi-religious and multi-racial society. This came to an end with forced conversions and harassment of Jews in the late 14th century, the establishment of the Spanish Inquisition in 1478, and the defeat of the last Moorish king in Spain and the official expulsion of all remaining Jews, both in 1492.

Her inner guides (a trusted source "committee") were telling her that her purpose was to carry this message to the rest of us: that the world of today must understand that people of different faiths can coexist peacefully and that they already have! I am moved to tears now writing this, as I was when she first explained this to me, though it has been years since I led her meditation.

Method 9: Hypnotherapy

Hypnotherapy refers to a broad grouping of techniques that involve hypnotizing the subject, thereby placing the ego in a state where it is much more capable of receiving messages from the unconscious. Hypnotherapy is used for a variety of things, for example, quitting smoking, losing weight, or dealing with psychological problems. Hypnotherapy is traditionally one of the most common facilitated methods for finding people's life purpose.

Hypnotherapists undergo a specific training program and receive a certification. Make sure that you check the credentials of any hypnotherapist if you plan to hire them. Hypnotizing people is not a procedure for amateurs. This method has the advantage of being one of the few facilitated methods that is regulated. In many countries, laws and certification boards ensure that hypnotherapists receive the proper training before being able to start their practice.

The resources in the Appendix include specific websites you can use to learn about hypnotherapy and find certified hypnotherapists. Traditionally, when hypnotherapy is used to find life purpose, this is done in the context of past life regression. Past life regression is a process of returning the subject to a time before they were born in this lifetime. This could either be a previous lifetime or a time between lives (after dying and before being born the next time). Obviously, this methodology presumes a belief in reincarnation. This can be problematic, as it excludes many people who do not believe in reincarnation.

Another disadvantage of this method is that many practitioners of it view life purpose as the solving of issues or problems left over from other lifetimes. This is a defect-oriented view; that is, it treats our life purpose as a problem to be solved rather than a gift to be manifested. This is an inherently ego-based viewpoint because the soul does not see us as problems and does not view us as flawed in any way. It is only through the eyes of the ego that we are flawed, have problems, or require fixing.

Hypnotherapy is similar to guided meditation in that the practitioner inducts and leads the client through a series of suggested images or experiences, often resulting in conversations with aspects of the psyche. It differs from guided meditation in that most hypnotherapists receive far more specific and prolonged training and can take clients into a deeper altered state than a typical guided meditation. Like guided meditation, it has very high success rates.

Method 10: Dream Work

This is effectively the same method as Method 6: Dreaming, except that you do it with the assistance of a trained dream interpreter. Dreams are the most direct access possible to the unconscious, so working with your dreams can provide an extraordinary window into your deeper psyche. Many people I know have done dream work for years, deepening in their understanding of themselves and reclaiming lost aspects of their psyche.

Unlike hypnotherapy, dream interpretation is not regulated and does not require certification. There are many different schools of thought on dream interpretation, some of which are very useful and many of which are not. In particular, any dream work methodology that ascribes specific and unchanging meanings to symbols and dreams should be avoided. You can easily find books that list meanings of dream symbols, much the way a dictionary lists definitions of words. They might look something like this:

> Bird: freedom
>
> Water: feelings, the unconscious
>
> Flying: inflation, arrogance

Avoid any book or dream work practitioner who operates in this kind of cookie-cutter way. Dream symbols are complex and can have multiple meanings, even within a single dream. The same image or symbol in one person's dream could mean something completely different if it showed up in someone else's dream. For this reason, dream work is a complex art form and requires years of training to learn properly.

Jungian analysts tend to be excellent dream work practitioners. There are also schools and workshops that teach dream work. Check the resources in the Appendix to learn about schools of dream work and where you can find a qualified dream interpreter.

As I mentioned earlier, dreaming is among the least efficient means of carrying on conversations with your trusted source because you can only ask one question per night. Asking more than one question tends to produce a confused dream response. You have little or no control in your dreams, so asking for a dream about your purpose may provide a dream about something else.

Some people have a very active mind that interferes with their attempts to find their purpose. If you have done a thorough job of clearing a path through your ego and you still can't quiet your mind when using other methods, dream work can be a good way to access your purpose. While you are dreaming, your ego has very little opportunity to interfere. When the ego does interfere in this method, it typically does so by making sure that you don't write your dream down so you'll forget it.

There is one situation in which learning to interpret dream symbols, or working with someone who already knows how, is absolutely necessary. Some people's trusted sources communicate only through symbols and images. This means that even if you make contact using another method, such as meditation or active imagination, you may have difficulty understanding what your trusted source is saying because it is speaking metaphorically rather than literally.

If your trusted source speaks in symbols and images, dream work may be the best possible way for you to learn to communicate with it. In my experience, roughly 10% of people have trusted sources that speak only in symbols and images, regardless of the method they use. If your trusted source speaks to you in literal, ordinary language, learning dream work to understand it is unnecessary. Consider yourself lucky.

Example

Elizabeth Scanzani is a coach who is trained in finding people's purpose. She also leads groups and workshops about dreams. She participated as a member of the staff at the Know Your Purpose Workshop, helping participants find their purpose. I encourage the coaches who work on staff to take the opportunity to deepen their understanding of their own purpose, so she asked for a dream to understand the specific steps of her blessing. Fortunately, she had a dream in which the specific steps of her blessing were listed out in writing. Unfortunately, she fell asleep again before she wrote them down! A few weeks later she asked for another dream, and she received several that night. There were four different dream segments.

SEGMENT ONE:

"I take a heating pad off my belly because someone will be coming on rounds to do an inspection. I don't want to get caught with it, so I take it off. My bedmate actually unplugs the heating pad, so hopefully it won't look like we were using it."

SEGMENT TWO:

"I get called out on an assignment. I'm a cop and kind of new at it. There's a criminal, a perpetrator, in the backseat and my job is to put my hand on his hand and hold him in place energetically. It has to be done a certain way, almost like a crisscross across his knuckles, so that when he presses up on my hand it takes all of the pressure. My hand doesn't move, fall over, or stick or anything.

"I'm a bit nervous; the criminal is into a sort of cultish crazy religion. My partner, who is a more experienced cop, is driving the police car. He can actually quote lots of stuff from this particular religious story, which he does. He really engages and earns trust with the convict in the backseat.

"This part of the dream repeats itself. I wonder who is going to watch my young child, because obviously I won't be able to do it myself if I'm out. I try to just remember that when I did this before, there was someone who was there to watch her, so it must still be the case, even though I'm doing it a little bit differently this time. This time, I think I'll know better what to do with the convict, too."

SEGMENT THREE:

"I have a close encounter with Frank, a spiritual teach of mine. He comes over to give me a hug. He flips me way up high above him, energetically. He knew just what to do for me. I might have thought I'd have trouble staying up there, but I am surprised that I didn't. I'm very balanced. I feel so good in my body, so strong, and it feels awesome to be balanced this way. He's done this to more and more people, and I am amazed at his strength!"

SEGMENT FOUR:

"The authorities are coming. I'm able to slip away behind some curtains, just in time. The guy I'm with and some other people are neatly tucked into what looks like sleeping bags turned on their ends, feet down. They're stuck onto a moving wall, vertically. It's like they're tucked in up to their necks with just their heads showing. They're moving to the right and I slip behind the left side of a curtain. It reminds me a bit of the Wizard of Oz... the man behind the curtain. The authorities look like WWII German or English soldiers: plain, maybe army green or gray uniforms, no insignia. I'm grateful for being assisted and allowed to slip away."

These dreams are much more difficult to interpret than the first dream Beth had. Fortunately, Beth teaches dream work and leads dream groups, so she is skilled at interpreting symbolic information. Within the images, she found information about the steps of her blessing, as well as other, more general instructions from her trusted source:

BLESSING STEPS:

Recall that the blessing is a process that has steps. Beth could do her blessing with an individual or with a group. These steps are written assuming she is doing them with an individual man.

1. Hold the person energetically.

2. Meet him where he is.

3. Engage and earn his trust.

4. Establish a close personal connection.

5. Balance the energies.

6. Mirror and reflect who he really is.

7. Hold him with strength so he can see and feel his strength.

8. Help him feel balanced and safe in his body.

9. Help him see that he can do more than he thought and feel better than he ever knew.

10. Move him into consciousness.

11. When the work is done, send him off and slip away.

You may have trouble seeing this information when you read the dreams above; don't worry. It's not at all obvious, which is what makes dream interpretation challenging and interesting. Symbols can convey a great deal of information. The interpretation of dreams and symbols is a skill that requires training to achieve.

Method 11: Journey Work

Many indigenous cultures around the world have rich traditions of journey work. Journey work has been used for thousands of years in initiation rituals, marine navigation, healing, and divination ("divining" the answers to questions and gaining insight into problems). The two most common forms used today are drum journeys and medicine journeys.

Drum journeys involve the rhythmic beating of a drum in conjunction with a form of guided meditation to take the journeyer into a dreamlike state. In this state, the journeyer "travels" to different realms and meets with spirits in the form of animals, people, or semi-human beings. Some observers believe that the journey is simply a meditative process that tricks the ego and thereby allows direct access to inner wisdom. Practitioners, however, often believe that the totems they encounter are wise and compassionate spirits from other planes of reality.

In a medicine journey, the journeyer is prescribed "medicine" (psychotropic substances) that will cause the dreamlike state to occur. Some shamanic traditions believe that the spirit of the plant from which the medicine is derived is a teacher and a source of wisdom.

Although there are few issues with drum journeys, medicine journeys have significant disadvantages. The principal disadvantage is legal. Many states, provinces, and countries prohibit the use of the psychotropic substances used in journey work. It is your responsibility to understand your national and local ordinances and to determine whether any particular substance is legal where you live. Some people solve this problem by traveling to countries where journey work is practiced traditionally and these substances are legal.

Another significant disadvantage is that of risk to health. The consumption of some psychotropic substances can have physical and psychological side effects, even if administered properly and only used once. Risks vary widely from one substance to another, however, so it pays to do some research.

It may require a series of journeys over a period of weeks, months, and possibly even years for you to develop a clear understanding of your purpose. Most journey work does not have understanding life purpose as its intent. In short, I would say that journey work is not the most efficient facilitated method for finding your life purpose.

That said, I know a number of people for whom other methods have not worked, but journey work has given them a clear understanding of their purpose. They speak very highly of it and are grateful for the understanding and transformation that they've achieved using this process.

The journeys themselves create experiences that raise awareness of core beliefs. Over time, this has the effect of bringing ego resistance and barriers to awareness and enabling their dissolution. This reorganization of the ego's structure not only creates permission for finding purpose, but a better platform from which to implement and manifest it. People I know who do journey work speak fondly of how repeated journeys have changed their outlook on life and brought them into contact with deeper truths.

Usually, journey work is led according to the belief systems of the native tradition in which the practitioner was trained. This can include things, such as animal spirit guides, that may fall outside of your religious belief system. If you're concerned about this, you can check with your journey practitioner before engaging in a relationship to make sure that the spiritual frame that they're using is compatible with yours.

Note that I have placed journey work among the facilitated methods. A bunch of people lying around in a room consuming mushrooms is not journey work. True journey work requires oversight by a trained facilitator. Journey work practitioners typically undergo years of shamanic training before they lead journeys. While individual traditions have their own techniques for qualifying journey work practitioners, I am not aware of any regulating boards or certifications.

Try drum journeying, unless your belief system contradicts that of the journey work practitioner. Note that, for some, it takes a number of attempts before having a successful drum journey. Stick with it.

If you are having trouble with ego resistance, you can try medicine journeys, but only do so with great care. Check the laws in your country and municipality; if the substances that will be used are illegal, you can travel to a place where they are legal. Research their health side effects so that you can make an informed choice. Ensure that your facilitator is a fully trained journey work practitioner, not just someone dispensing recreational drugs.

Whether you try drum journeys or medicine journeys, let your facilitator know that you are seeking information about your life's purpose.

Example

My friend Matthew is one of several people I know who have successfully used journey work to find their purpose. Since being told he needed to declare a major in college, Matthew had been haunted by trying to find his purpose. He tried many different methods to no avail. In the example below, he used the medicine journey method, as opposed to drum journeys, to find his purpose. Here's what Matthew has to say about how he did this:

"I was introduced to plant medicine, which is one of many shamanic methods. My plant medicine guides were also trained as therapists in a beautiful somatic psychotherapy method. The medicine of the plants provided revelation of what is possible; the somatic therapy provided the integration and means to bring the acquired healing and wisdom into my daily life.

"There is so much that is so personal that emerges from doing plant medicine journeys. And relative to purpose and finding purpose, I would say this: Plant medicine journeys provide the opportunity to examine one's sense of self, to shed outdated beliefs, to own and revel in our own beauty, and to unlayer and to unfold into an authentic, unfettered self and Self.

"And so in one of my early plant medicine journeys, having entered the dreamy realms and realities unique to that particular plant, I encountered a haunted mansion built from my limiting beliefs and my fears. This haunted mansion was compelling me to enter, sucking me in, knowing I would likely die not far from the limen of the doorway. As I stepped through the door's threshold, I faced a bright light, a clear whitish-blue space. This light illuminated the two-by-four supports that were holding up the façade of a scary, haunted mansion. And while in that space, I was released from all fears and doubts. I could still find them, feel them, but I was no longer constrained by them. And in this space, I found possibility and imagination of 'self.'

"One of these beliefs was that I would find meaning in some vocational destiny into which I was born to live, if only I could find it. And this belief, on the face of it, meant that I would only find a purposeful way of being in the aspect of my life that earned a living. And as each fear dissolved, wisdom emerged in its place. A piece of this wisdom was my own: the wisdom of 'Oh, this is who I am.' Another piece of the wisdom I received came from the plant-spirit itself: 'Here are your missing experiences and resources that bring you closer to wholeness.' The last piece of wisdom came from a divine source, so beautifully revealed by the plant: 'Here is where you come from, why your life is already perfect, and knowledge of your way and how to stay on your path.'

"Layer by layer I was healed of my doubts, fears, and sources of self-limitation. As each layer dissipated, a gift of release and wisdom always emerged: A portion of who I am, safely cocooned away until I was ready, was revealed and reclaimed. The plant's spirit and wisdom taught me how to live into my expanded self with integrity and courage. Eventually, I came to my own personal understanding that there is no purpose in life other than to remember who we are and from where we ultimately come. And with that remembrance in hand, I have free will to surrender to and follow a divinely inspired path already laid out, perfectly, before me. And this, too, has become a part of my purpose.

"Eventually, I felt ready and asked for guidance on how best to apply my life in service to the creative force that informs all moments—current, past, and future. In the two journeys where I specifically asked for guidance on my purpose, after first proving myself trustworthy, I earned the right to choose to be a guardian of and a conduit for this life force. An image provided in a journey serves to remind me of this choice and the rewards and responsibilities that go with it. The image is of a warrior, with sword raised and ready, standing on the edge of the current moment. The warrior is witness to the purity of the life force that runs through all moments. He protects this pure thread. He protects it from fear and self-indulgence, especially his own. He stands ready, asking what way of being, what action will most serve this moment, constantly searching for his own fears and indulgences that might compel action without integrity, thereby preparing himself to be a pure conduit for selfless action in service to the moment and in integrity with his path and sense of self. In this way, self and Self become integral. Norman Maclean, the author of *A River Runs Through It,* said it beautifully in the closing paragraph of his book: '…and all things become one and a river runs through it.'

"I accepted life's invitation, took the path laid at my feet, and started training in the ways of a plant medicine guide. I began acquiring the training and tools to be a more capable guardian and conduit of the life force, the river that runs through all. In the moment of this choice, I also knew that I did not yet know in what concrete way I would be of service to this earth-bound reality. A year has passed since my choice. And true to the image of the warrior, I have stayed aware of the myriad ways in which I am being guided on my path.

"When Tim invited me to contribute my example to this book, I found myself wishing my stated purpose were more concrete, more actionable.

We had a short session in which Tim taught me about his concepts of essence, blessing, and mission, and it really resonated with me. I used his exploratory questions and method to prepare for a journey that I took just before this book went to print. These are the three questions I chose to take into the journey with me:

- ✓ 'Is there a purpose to be known?' (I already knew the answer to this, but it never hurts to ask.)
- ✓ 'What compels me toward this purpose?'
- ✓ 'What prevents me from choosing and acting on my purpose?'

"The medicine I used is one that helps dissolve the ego without dissolving my sense of this reality. This allows my own innate truth and clarity to emerge in direct relationship with the questions and longings I hold in this reality. And as the medicine took hold, I felt a huge wave of anxiety build in my heart and then in my belly. I have learned to trust these moments, knowing that the anxiety is a beacon of further wisdom and wholeness. In my response to my commenting on my anxiousness, my medicine guide lit a stick of Chinese Moxibustion (essentially a stick of herbs to burn). Under the warmth of the Moxibustion and the smell of the herbs, my anxiousness transformed into the familiar remembrance of love, pure love, that is powerfully healing, fiercely courageous, and uncompromising in my acceptance of it and in its acceptance of me.

"I remember the multitude of times I have been here before in journeys. I feel how much love has permeated my present day-to-day life. Then I feel my love for my parents. And I feel the shadowy remnants of the protecting fear that I will lose my essential self in the normal, crazy process of being a child. This fear protected me by keeping certain aspects of life out and certain aspects of me in. One such aspect is the love from my parents and my love of them. As I accepted and really metabolized their love for me and mine for them, the answers to my questions gracefully emerged and even filled in the blanks of my purpose:

✓ My essence is pure, fierce love.

✓ My blessing is knowing and living the truth of love, which informs and transforms what I create and accept in this life.

✓ My mission is to guide myself and those who choose to engage with me in illuminating and transforming those aspects of our self that impede the awakening to and acceptance of our own unique truth and experience of self-love and its connection to God.

"'What's love got to do with it?' Everything."

It took Matthew several years and many journeys to achieve the level of clarity he currently enjoys about his life's purpose. According to all those I've spoken to about it, this is often the case with journey work. Note how important it was for him to enter the journey with clear questions about his purpose!

Many thanks for the help I received on this chapter from Richard Whiteley, best-selling author of *The Corporate Shaman*. Since I am not trained in journey work, I consulted Richard, who has trained in shamanic practices for 16 years. Richard uses shamanic techniques in his consulting work with top leaders and corporations.

> *"We must be willing to get rid of
> the life we planned so as to have
> the life that is waiting for us."*
>
> – Joseph Campbell

Chapter Eight

Interpreting Your Results

This chapter is for interpreting the communications that you've received from a trusted source. At this point you've used one or more
of the direct access methods and had some kind of communication.
You may not be sure whether you were actually communicating with
a trusted source, and you may be uncertain about what it all means.
If you've been unable to make contact with anything, it is not time to
read this chapter yet. Go back and try other methods, particularly the
facilitated ones, to see if you can make contact with a trusted source.
If you're unable to make contact, read Chapter 10: I Didn't Find My
Purpose—What's Up?

Some of the information you've received may be confusing to you,
and you may not be sure whether it is authentic or not. This is normal;
hang in there. Go through this process and see what you get. There is
a specific order to the questions and exercises in the interpretation process. Please stick with it and go through these steps. I'm doing things in
this order based on my experience working with hundreds of people.

If you have made contact with a trusted source or something that might be a trusted source, my first and most important recommendation is to take a break. I find it usually works to take as long as a week after making contact before trying to make any decisions or do anything with what you've learned. This may seem long, but it can take the ego a lot of time to absorb the new information. Often, after particularly direct contact with the trusted source, people can experience fatigue, confusion, skepticism, and mental distraction. This is completely normal; expect it and give yourself time. If you've waited a significant period of time, roughly a week, it is time to start making meaning of what you've received.

Was This Real?

It is entirely normal during and after making contact with a trusted source to have a skeptical reaction. By "skeptical reaction" I mean that you find yourself asking questions like, "Was this real? Was that really my trusted source? How can I tell?" You may also be experiencing active disbelief, that is, hearing a voice in your head saying something like, "This cannot possibly be real. I made this up. I'm just telling myself what I want to hear."

This is what I'm calling a skeptical reaction. It is entirely normal and happens to nearly everyone. I've only met two types of people for whom skeptical reactions don't occur. The first type is people with very strong spiritual or religious beliefs who have made repeated contact with a trusted source in the past. The second type is people who have spent years in spiritual practices, such as meditation and prayer, to such a degree that they have completely transformed their ego. Everybody else has a skeptical reaction. I don't fit into either of these categories, so I frequently have skeptical reactions, too.

A skeptical reaction is not an indicator that it was a real connection, nor is it an indicator that it wasn't. When people connect to something that isn't a trusted source and get inaccurate information, they have a skeptical reaction because their inner Skeptic doubts the accuracy of the information, and rightly so. When people make an authentic connection to a trusted source and get accurate information, their inner Skeptic reacts to an unfamiliar experience and information coming from an unknown source. *A skeptical reaction doesn't tell you whether the source and the information are authentic;* it only tells you that you have a properly functioning inner Skeptic.

After you have connected to what might have been a trusted source, the first decision you have to make is whether or not what you experienced was real. This is why a skeptical reaction is the first thing that comes up. It is your Skeptic offering you the appropriate question for you to examine. Unfortunately, there is no way to conclusively prove or disprove that any communication you've received from a trusted source is authentic. It just doesn't work like that. This is an internal experience; it cannot be measured and weighed and, therefore, it cannot be proven, nor can it be disproven. What this means is that the choice of whether or not to believe that this was authentic communication is just that: a choice.

Every choice has consequences. If you choose to believe that this was (or might have been) an authentic communication, then there is more work to do. Specifically, you will need to make meaning of what you've received, decide what to do about it, and test it to see if it improves your life. If you don't believe that this was an authentic communication, then you can either go back to try to get an authentic communication or abandon the effort.

An interesting feature of choices, particularly choices of belief, is that they are self-reinforcing. What I mean is that if you choose not to believe that this was true, then your mind will automatically provide evidence to demonstrate the accuracy of your choice. You will be able to find flaws in this book, the process, and what you've received. This will reinforce your belief that it wasn't real. You will put down this book and go back to live in a world that appears random and not being guided by any specific purpose or plan. This is fine, normal, and how most people choose to live.

If, on the other hand, you choose to believe that this communication was real, then you will tend to make choices that support that belief. You will probably choose to do things that are purposeful and to avoid things that are not. Living that way will create the experience of having a purposeful life. Therefore, your choice to believe that it was true and that you do have a purpose will reinforce itself over time. You will have the experience of moving forward in a world that has a plan and where you are on a path (though your doubts may never go away completely). This is a perfectly normal and acceptable choice. Either way is fine. It is up to you which way to go.

At this point you are probably not prepared to make this choice. You are probably still asking, "But, Tim, how do I tell whether it was real?" The next section talks about how to evaluate whether or not the source that gave you the information was legitimate. But first, I wanted to be very clear with you that the decision about whether or not what you experienced was real is entirely up to you. And no one but you can make that decision, because you are the one who will live with the consequences.

Evaluating Your Trusted Source

When people use direct methods to talk to trusted sources, they frequently make connections and receive profound, life-altering information. But other things can happen as well. Parts of the ego may come in to answer the questions. These "impostors" may be accidental or deliberate. They can sometimes offer very plausible-sounding purpose information.

Fortunately, having worked with hundreds of people, I have found very distinct patterns that occur in authentic trusted sources, and equally distinct patterns that occur when "impostor" parts pose as trusted sources. We can use this information to evaluate your experience and help you decide whether to believe that it was authentic or not.

Here are the factors I recommend you use to determine whether you were communicating with an authentic trusted source:

1. The speech patterns of the source.

2. The effect of the experience on you.

3. Your feelings and intuition about the source and the information it revealed.

CHARACTERISTIC SPEECH PATTERNS

While trusted sources may use different language and styles to communicate, these characteristics are common:

1. Trusted sources use confident, declarative language; they don't beat around the bush. They say what's so, and they don't hesitate or apologize for it: "You need to relax and take it easy." "You were designed to help people who are in pain." The communication usually sounds like statements of fact and direct instructions.

2. Trusted sources usually don't use speculative language: "I think your purpose is to..." "You might be moving towards..." When you hear this kind of uncertainty, one of several things is probably true: You have a "noisy connection" to the source, you're asking about something too detailed for the trusted source to care about, or you have an impostor on the line.

3. Some things that the trusted source says, the ego just wouldn't say: "You're not ready to know your purpose yet." "You overestimate the importance of your work skills." If it says things that surprise you, this increases the chances that it is an authentic trusted source. Impostors are usually trying to "play it safe" and don't put forth radical new ideas or information. It is especially confirming evidence if the source says things you don't want to hear or don't want to be true.

4. Trusted sources play big picture, not small: "It will be years before you're ready for your real purpose." "It doesn't matter which job you take next; either one will lead you where you need to go." "I don't care which car you buy. Ask something else." Trusted sources are high-level strategists and often don't want to get into the details.

5. Trusted sources sometimes say "we" rather than "I": "We have been waiting for you to ask us about your purpose." "We under-stand how challenging this is for you; we're here to help you." Often this is *not* true for monotheistic people; if your trusted source is God, God will usually say "I" rather than "We." If a trusted source refers to itself as "I," this is neither confirming nor unconfirming evidence.

6. Trusted sources withhold information. They will often refuse to answer questions or remain completely silent and not answer at all. If this happens, just ask another question. This is a very good indicator of an authentic trusted source; impostors will try to answer every question you ask. Trusted sources are especially reluctant to reveal details of the mission: "You have a very big mission, but you're not ready to know what it is."

7. If you pursue questions that the trusted source has already said aren't timely, or questions regarding too great a level of detail, the trusted source will refuse to answer, become confused, or just stay silent. "I don't know what you should eat for lunch. Ask another question."

It is important to note that the converses of these aren't necessarily true. For example, a source that doesn't answer some questions is probably an authentic trusted source. That doesn't mean that a source that answers every question is an impostor! Likewise, a source that gets into details may be authentic. And if the source tells you things you already know and doesn't say anything surprising, that doesn't mean it's an impostor.

You need to look over the notes from your interaction with the trusted source and compare them to this list. Applying these criteria will give you some sense of the likelihood that it was authentic, but it is not an exact science. Fortunately, there are other criteria we can apply as well.

EFFECT ON YOU

Regardless of what information you received (if any), a connection with a trusted source has a characteristic effect. This will be true even if the source refused to disclose your purpose, so long as there was a sufficiently direct and prolonged interaction. You will typically feel more at ease, more serene and peaceful, and that something is "holding" you. Another common reaction is feeling drained, distracted, and introspective. At the beginning of the process, people are often agitated and needing (even desperate for) guidance and purpose. This agitation will dissipate and relax when a genuine connection occurs (although you may feel frustrated if some desired information was withheld).

Sometimes the experience can be one of revelation. I have seen people burst into tears with relief and joy when they realize that they are not alone in the universe, that something is watching over them. The experience can be profound and life changing. It can also feel overwhelming, as if you've learned more than you can handle. These strong feelings are compelling evidence that the connection and the source were authentic and, therefore, that the information you received was authentic as well.

Although revelation is wonderful when it happens, it doesn't happen for everyone! For some, the connection is a simple accessing of deep truth, with a sense of knowing but little strong emotion. People are different, and so are their reactions.

What were you feeling during and right after your interaction with the trusted source? Were you elated? Drained? Frightened? Rattled? Confused? Calm and peaceful? Overwhelmed? Any of these reactions is evidence that the connection was authentic. If you felt no different, then the connection may not have been authentic.

There are exceptions to this. I have clients who have spoken to God every day for years. They come to me to find their purpose, and I send them back to God with questions. They may not have strong reactions from connecting to God. Does this mean it wasn't real? No! It's just nothing new; they do it every day! A connection with a trusted source has a much stronger effect on you if it is an unfamiliar experience. You are also less likely to have a strong reaction if you already have a sense of your purpose and the connection with your trusted source confirms that you were correct. New and surprising information provokes a stronger reaction.

Remember, usually there will be skeptical reaction ("Was this real?"), but this happens whether or not it was a trusted source. Skepticism doesn't tell you whether the connection was real or not.

YOUR INTUITION

Your inner sense of whether this was real or not is probably the best indicator of all. What do your feelings tell you? What does your gut tell you? People often just "know" whether their connection was real, with no reason or logic.

Note that this is very different from what you "think." Your mind is a magnificent machine, and it will produce thoughts, doubts, criteria, reasons, and so on. These have great value, but I am speaking of something else. Intuition is different from reason; it is a sense of knowing that doesn't require evidence. If you don't have access to such an inner sense of knowing, that's fine. Use your judgment and the criteria above to make your decision.

Now that you have read all of these criteria, it is time to choose. Do you believe that you connected to a trusted source? Do you believe what it told you? Your call, yes or no.

If you're still not sure, you don't have to make an absolute decision. You could decide instead whether it probably was or probably wasn't a trusted source. You could assume it was a trusted source and "test-drive" the information you received. The criteria we just discussed are one way of determining the validity. There are two other ways we will explore later, but they require some purpose information to work with. If you are still unsure, I recommend that you continue to work with this source and this information. We will be able to do more validation once we've worked more with the information you received.

If you're reasonably certain that you weren't communicating with an authentic trusted source, or if you weren't able to make contact at all, skip ahead to Chapter 10: I Didn't Find My Purpose—What's Up? If you believe you were (or might have been) communicating with a trusted source and you received any information at all, keep reading.

Interpreting the Information

If you've had an interaction with a trusted source, you might be confused by some of the things it said. This is very common. You might also be frightened or intimidated by what it told you. This is common, too. Take a deep breath and hang in there!

The next few exercises will help you to make meaning of what you received. They will also help you to decide what, if anything, to do about it.

The first step is to divide up what you received into categories. Trusted sources can say a lot of profound things in a very short period of time, and our minds have trouble keeping up. Also, some of the ego defenders can become agitated, making it even harder to think clearly.

I find it very useful to categorize the communication from your trusted source into the following "buckets":

1. Purpose Information – This category includes information about your essence, blessing, and mission. It also includes anything the

trusted source said about your fundamental nature and design. For example, "You are an angel of God." "You are a lighthouse." "You are an instrument of great power." "You are meant to advise powerful leaders."

2. Instructions – These are specific things the trusted source told you to do. Examples include: "Play the flute." "Love your children and give them what they need to thrive." "Move to Arizona." "Don't leave your company yet; you're not ready." Put broad and sweeping instructions, like, "Heal the pain of the world," or "Help African-American women to empower themselves," in the Purpose Information category; they are missions.

3. Information – Your trusted source may say other things that don't fit into either of the previous categories. Capture this information as a third category. Examples include: "You will meet a soul mate soon." "Your business partner is more concerned than she admits." "The world is waiting for you to bring your message!" These are neither purpose information nor instructions, but are often very useful nonetheless.

Once you have broken up what the trusted source said into these three categories, we can start to analyze it and make meaning of what you received. Take some time now to create these three categories and sort the information from your trusted source. This will be easier to do if you took notes on a computer; you can copy and paste the information into categories.

Instructions

Look first at the list of instructions. What were you told to do? This is one of those moments when you need to exercise your free will. You do not have to follow all of the instructions! You *do* need to decide which ones to follow, though. It can help to have some criteria to use when you are trying to decide. Here are some questions you might ask yourself when evaluating each instruction:

✓ "Will it be safe for me to do this?"

✓ "Will I enjoy it?"

✓ "Will I grow and develop as a result?"

✓ "Does it feel like something I should do?"

✓ "Do I have what I need to do this?"

✓ "What impact will it have on my life?"

✓ "What impact will it have on other people?"

✓ "What help, if any, will I need?"

Underline the instructions you will follow. For each one, you must decide how to do it. Do you need to schedule something in your calendar? Do you need support from someone else, such as your spouse, boss, a coach, or a company? Is it something you will need to practice every day? Write down the steps you will need to take to follow this instruction. If you're not clear, go back and ask more questions of your trusted source. Trusted sources often have excellent suggestions for how to follow their instructions.

Let's work with an example. Imagine that you received this instruction: "Meditate every day for at least 20 minutes." After some thought, you decide to commit to meditating at least five times a week for 20 minutes. When will you do this? You need to pick a time and schedule it in your calendar. You may need to talk to your spouse to make sure that you will have the time available and that other things won't intrude on your meditation time. Do you also need to set some kind of reminder or alarm? How will you be sure that it actually happens? Do you need someone else to check up on you?

Okay, now imagine that you have no idea how to meditate, but you got this instruction. You need to learn! Meditation training for beginners is available in most cities these days, so you'll need to check a course catalog, yoga center, or adult learning center for a suitable class. If you find more than one, check with your trusted source to see which one is right for you.

Get the picture? Look at the list of steps you wrote down. Will your plan actually get this to happen? You know yourself and your schedule; be realistic. If not, what other steps or support do you need? Write it down!

Do this for each instruction. If you find it overwhelming, you might need to cut back on the number of instructions you commit to following. Remember, you do not need to follow every instruction in order to live a purposeful life. But following none of them won't get the job done! The most important thing to do is pick something you know you can do and get started. Don't allow yourself to become overwhelmed and do nothing.

Inner Work and Practices

Some instructions have more to do with your behavior and beliefs. If you get an instruction like, "Be honest with the people in your life," or "Make peace with the possibility of failure," then it isn't exactly an activity you can schedule in your calendar or check off your to-do list! You will need to convert this instruction into something specific that you can do.

In my experience, the best way to do this is something called a "practice." A practice is a way of setting up a different behavior for yourself in a very specific way. You set a goal for a new behavior, then you measure your progress towards that goal.

I once had a trusted source tell a client in a Voice Dialogue session that she should play the flute. (She already knew how, but hadn't done it in years.) The trusted source was trying to get her in touch with her creative side and to give her a way to relax and shift out of her busy, working mindset.

"Play the flute" is a very clear instruction, but it's not very specific. In order to make it specific, you'd have to know some other things: How often will you play it and for how long? Will you play the flute alone or in front of other people? How will you remember to do it?

Here's what a practice about playing the flute might look like: "I will play the flute for 15 minutes, three times a week. I will put appointments in my calendar at 8:15-8:30AM on Monday, Wednesday, and Friday. If I miss a session, I will play on Saturday morning to make it up."

Much more specific than "play the flute," isn't it? This is something that might actually happen. It isn't actually that important whether you actually play for exactly 45 minutes every week; the intention and the structure result in a lot more flute-playing than would happen if you did what most people do, which sounds more like this: "Yeah, my trusted source is right; it would be great if I played the flute more often. I should really make more time to do that." Good luck with that! That sort of vague intention usually results in exactly nothing.

Let's take a more challenging example. Let's say your trusted source gave you an instruction to change some habit or behavior of yours, something that isn't so easy. Imagine you were told, "You need to tell the truth in your relationships." Some people are naturally conflict-averse and will withhold their true feelings in order to "keep the peace." Well, telling the truth in relationships is easier said than done! First let's look at the vague version. What would happen if this were your plan? "Yeah, you're right, I hold back too much. I really should say what I'm feeling. I'll make an effort to do that."

If you're lucky, you'll remember this intention for a few hours. How often will you tell the truth? To whom? How will you remember to do it? Who will support you? Here's what a more specific practice might look like: "I will tell an uncomfortable truth to someone in my life at least three times per week. One of those must be with either my boss or my husband. At 6PM on Friday, I will write in my journal about the times I did it and what it felt like, and what happened. I will set an alarm on my watch that will go off at 6PM Friday to remind me. I will set up a marquee screensaver on my computer that reads, 'Have you told the truth today?' I will also tell Jen about what I'm doing and talk about it with her every week during our Tuesday morning coffee."

Now you have a shot! Reminders, other people in your life who will support you, specific numbers of times to do it, journaling: All of these things increase the chances that the practice will stick. Eventually it will become second nature (a new "habit") and you will no longer need to track it so carefully. Expect that to take about 90 days.

Exercise: Changing Your Behavior

Take one of the instructions that your trusted source gave you, one that requires you to change your behavior or develop a new habit. Answer the following questions about it:

1. How will you do this?

2. How often?

3. With whom?

4. How will you remember to do it?

5. Who could support you in doing it?

6. How and when will you record your progress and your learning?

7. What specific things do you need to do to get started? (e.g., conversations you need to have, reminders you need to create or schedule, etc.)

Wait, we're not quite done yet. When people create practices, they often create practices that won't actually work. Let's say you're going to pray regularly, so you set up a practice to pray every day for 30 minutes in the evening, right before bed. Well, how realistic is that? Often these kinds of intentions are set by a part of us that is telling us what we "should" do, not what we're actually capable of doing or likely to do. For example, you might hear your inner Critic saying, "Come on, you have to meditate every day! And for at least 40 minutes, otherwise it doesn't count. Fred meditates at least that long." Or something to that effect. If you don't catch this internal process in action, you might set an unrealistic goal for yourself. Now when you don't meet it, you will probably feel bad about yourself and abandon the whole project, or flog yourself into doing it. It's much easier to set a simple goal, something you know you can do, and start there. Then you can expand it later, if you wish.

Okay, review your practice. Is it realistic? Is it something you're actually likely to do, or is it too ambitious? Do you need more support from others or additional reminders? Revise it, making it something you genuinely believe you are capable of.

Now you need to implement it: Talk to the people who will support you, create your appointments, reminders, or alarms, and write your practice down where you can find it easily. Go for it! Once you get the hang of this, you can have two or three practices at a time. I don't recommend more than that, and make sure you're doing well with one practice before you create a second one.

Purpose Information

The other type of information you receive from your trusted source is purpose information. When your trusted source reveals purpose information, it may be very obviously about your purpose, for example, "Your essence is feminine radiance and feminine power." The source is speaking directly about your essence, your blessing, or your mission.

Sometimes it is harder to tell whether it is purpose information or not. Following are two other types of statements that should go in the "Purpose Information" category.

Descriptions of Your Design – Sometimes the trusted source will make statements about how you were made or what you were made for: "You are designed to be able to see the possibility, the potential, what is there that other people can't see." "You're meant to teach others that they have all of the special capabilities and qualities they need to fulfill their mission."

Sweeping Instructions – Some instructions are so vast in scope that they boggle the mind. Something like "meditate more often" makes sense in a day-to-day context, as does "stop worrying so much about what your mother thinks." But instructions like "solve the world's food and energy problems" and "bring the sacred trust back into business" go far beyond one individual. These are actually missions, so include them in the "Purpose Information" category, not the "Instructions" category.

Next you will need to sort the purpose information into its three aspects: essence, blessing, and mission.

ESSENCE

Recall that your essence is your fundamental being state. When trusted sources talk about your essence, they will often say, "You are..." Here are some things I've heard trusted sources say to people about their essence:

- ✓ "You are a beacon of joy."
- ✓ "You are the Sword of Truth."
- ✓ "You are an angel of God."

Pick out statements that speak about who and what you are, not about what you do. Don't edit them; just rewrite them under the heading "Essence."

BLESSING

Your blessing is a process. As such, it is something you do, over and over again. You do your blessing with individuals and possibly also with groups of people. Pick out everything that describes this process: what you do, for whom you do it, how it works, and what effect it has. You may need to go back and ask more questions of your trusted source to fully explore your blessing. Reread "Asking Good Questions" in Chapter 5 (see page 78) to understand which questions you should ask. Gather together all of the information your trusted source gave you about your blessing and rewrite it under the heading "Blessing."

MISSION

Information about your mission is often phrased as an instruction that is sweeping in scope and impact. It's something you could only do once, like "raise the world to a new level of consciousness" or "solve the world's food and energy problems." You may feel overwhelmed, queasy, or inadequate when presented with your mission. Don't worry, you don't have to do it now, you only need to rewrite it under the heading "Mission." Keep breathing!

Now that you have sorted all of the information from your trusted source, continue on to Chapter 9: Creating Purpose Statements. If you didn't make contact with a trusted source, you can go back and try again or keep reading for more help.

> *"Whatever is at the center of our life will be the source of our security, guidance, wisdom, and power."*
>
> – Stephen Covey

Chapter Nine

Creating Purpose Statements

The Role of Purpose Statements

The reason to have a purpose statement is to be able to quickly and simply connect you to your purpose. The purpose statement itself is not your purpose; it is an approximation of your purpose rendered in words. Your purpose is the most fundamental aspect of your being and defies language. If you have successfully used direct access methods to find your purpose, your purpose statement will remind you not only of your purpose, but also of the connection you achieved with your trusted source. A good purpose statement will bring up the feelings you had when you connected to your trusted source and the conversation that took place during that connection.

If you are trying to create a purpose statement based on indirect access methods only, there is a tremendous amount riding on the wording that you choose. This is not the best way to make a purpose statement.

With indirect access methods, you will have much less information to use compared to what you would have from successfully using direct access methods. In this situation, the ego tends to get very involved in wordsmithery, because the purpose statement is all you will have for understanding your purpose.

For these reasons, it is best to create purpose statements as a result of the successful use of direct access methods. If direct access methods didn't work for you, then you may not have that luxury. In that case, use the patterns you discovered during the Purpose Hunting exercise as the basis for your purpose statements.

Types of Purpose Statements

A purpose statement can be based on any aspect of your purpose: your essence, blessing, or mission. This means that a purpose statement can reflect either the being aspect of your purpose or the doing aspect. Because you may have an essence, a blessing, and potentially one or more missions, you may have more than one purpose statement. Even though we only have one purpose, it can sometimes be too confusing to the ego to look at the purpose as a single thing. Much like the blind men and the elephant, we will need to examine each aspect of your purpose separately, in order to better understand the whole.

Creating an essence-based purpose statement is relatively simple. An essence-based purpose statement usually begins with the words "I am." This is because essence speaks to being rather than doing.

The best way to create a blessing-based purpose statement is to first gain a full understanding of your blessing. This might take several conversations with your trusted source. What you are looking for is a complete understanding of the process that you do and how it affects other people. Included in this are the steps of the process, for whom the process is intended, and the before and after, that is, how the other person is affected by you doing this process. This may be confusing to you and it might take a little while to get it clearly articulated. It is well worth the effort, however, as you will likely derive the most immediate benefit from understanding this aspect of your purpose. This is because it speaks directly to the work that you do in the world and has significant applicability to your professional life.

It usually doesn't work to use the entire list of the steps of your blessing in the purpose statement. A blessing-based purpose statement is really a distillation or a simple articulation of the process that you do, rather than the entire process. Think of it as the title of the process.

A mission-based purpose statement is an articulation of the specific task that you are meant to do in the world or the impact that task is meant to achieve. Your trusted source can articulate your mission either in terms of what it is you're supposed to do or, more commonly, in terms of the larger goal it is supposed to achieve. Mission-based purpose statements can be confronting because it is often difficult for us to imagine that we could ever achieve this scale of impact. This is because the ego naturally assumes that it is going to have to do this alone, gets frightened, and feels inadequate. There may be hundreds, thousands, or even millions of people called to the same mission as you, although you may never meet them. Trusted sources have a tendency to coordinate these activities, even though the individuals themselves may be unaware of the connection.

Mission-based purpose statements often begin with, "My mission is to…" followed by the activity or goal the trusted source has asked for. At this stage, you don't need to worry about whether you're going to do this or how you're going to achieve it. All we are trying to do is get a clear understanding of what your trusted source is asking you to do.

Sample Purpose Statements

These are all actual purpose statements; a few are mine and the rest are from my coaching clients and workshop participants.

PURPOSE STATEMENTS BASED ON ESSENCE:

- ✓ "I am a gift of love."
- ✓ "I am the Sword of Truth."
- ✓ "I am a beacon of joy."

PURPOSE STATEMENTS BASED ON BLESSING:

- ✓ "My blessing is to connect people with their divinity."
- ✓ "My blessing is to show people their path."
- ✓ "My blessing is to create abundance and new possibilities."

Note that all of these articulate some kind of activity. This is because your blessing is one of the "doing" aspects of purpose.

PURPOSE STATEMENTS BASED ON MISSION:

- ✓ "My mission is to bring the sacred trust back into business."
- ✓ "My mission is to engage the nation in possibility."
- ✓ "My mission is to ease the world's pain."

These purpose statements articulate specific tasks that have been assigned to individuals as missions. Unlike the blessing-based purpose statements, they speak to some definite impact in the world, often on a huge scale. You can do your blessing over and over again, but once your mission is complete, it is done.

Creating Your Purpose Statements

Creating a purpose statement can be challenging. An accurate purpose statement can be a very confronting and vulnerable thing. I have seen clients burst into tears after saying their purpose statement out loud.

It helps to have the support of a trained coach or a trusted friend or relative in this process. A coach is often better because someone who is close to you may have a vested interest in you pursuing or not pursuing your purpose and may not be able to be objective.

One thing that causes the ego to prevent a good purpose statement from being created is its fears about how other people will react to your purpose. It is very important when you're creating your purpose statements not to consider how they will sound to others. The best way to do this is to make a temporary commitment not to disclose your purpose statement to anyone, except perhaps to one trusted advisor such as a coach. In this way, your ego can be relieved of having to worry about how the purpose statements will sound to anyone. Communicating your purpose is an entirely different activity that we will go into later in the book. For now, all we need to do is construct purpose statements that have the most meaning and feeling for you. They may make no sense to anyone else; that is fine. All that matters is that they elicit feelings in you and serve as reminders of your purpose.

The best indicator that you have created an accurate purpose statement is that you have an emotional or physical reaction to it when you say it out loud. The stronger the emotional or physical reaction, the better. It is important to realize that it doesn't matter what the emotion or physical reaction is. Feelings of joy and elation are strong indications of an accurate purpose statement; so are fear and panic. You may have heard the saying, "The opposite of love is not hate; it is indifference." Love and hate are both signs of a good purpose statement. Only the strength of the reaction matters, not the type of reaction.

Indifference is a sign of a bad purpose statement. When you have little or no feeling about your purpose statement, it is usually a sign that some aspect of the ego—usually an ego protector—has edited and censored all of the life out of it. It usually does this either to prevent you from having to confront your purpose or from facing the possibility of communicating your purpose to someone else. It's usually best to use the words exactly as they came from your trusted source. The more you edit and modify them, the further away you will get from your purpose.

Exercise: Create Your Purpose Statements

In this exercise, you will create a purpose statement for each aspect of your purpose. You may not have received information about your essence, blessing, or mission. Only use the sections for which you have information. It is common for people not to receive information about all three, especially on the first try.

Essence

If you have essence information from your trusted source, you can use it to create some purpose statements:

1. On a blank sheet of paper or computer document, write down the words "I am."

2. Now write down one or more of the words that your trusted source used to describe your essence. For example, if when you asked about your essence your trusted source said, "love and compassion," you could write down these possible purpose statements:

    "I am love."

    "I am compassion."

    "I am love and compassion."

3. Now try making some more purpose statements by adding words in the middle. Some sample sentence stems you can use are things like "I am an agent of," "I am a beacon of," "I am a gift of," followed by whatever words your trusted source used to describe your essence. Write down at least 3-4 different purpose statements using whatever words were given by your trusted source and different sentence stems. Make up some of your own; don't restrict yourself to these. This will result in some additional candidate purpose statements that look like this:

"I am a gift of love."

"I am a beacon of love."

"I am an agent of love."

4. If a friend or coach is helping you, have them suggest some options based on what your trusted source said. This is a brainstorm; the more options you can come up with, the better. Don't worry about whether they're accurate or not.

Now you should have at least 5-6 different possible essence-based purpose statements, and possibly many more than that. We'll choose the best one soon.

Blessing

If you have information about your blessing, seek to characterize the process that you do and those for whom you do it as simply and clearly as possible. Think of the purpose statement as a title that describes the process of your blessing. If you can, use words that your trusted source used. Remember that a blessing-based purpose statement should speak to an activity that you do rather than to who or what you are.

1. Start with the sentence stem "My blessing is to..." Avoid job titles and professions; your purpose is more fundamental than that.

2. Write down at least 3-5 different purpose statements that describe your blessing. You can write a few based on the activity and several more based on the impact your blessing has.

3. If a friend or coach is helping you, have them suggest some options based on what your trusted source said. Just like before, this is a brainstorm; the more options you can come up with, the better. Don't worry about whether they're accurate or not.

Mission

If your trusted source gave you a mission, you can create a mission-based purpose statement. In some ways, this is the easiest one to do.

1. Start with the sentence stem "My mission is to..."

2. Write down 3-5 different purpose statements as simply and clearly as possible, expressing the task that you have been sent to do in the world or the impact that you are meant to have. Use the words your trusted source said rather than making up new ones.

3. If a friend or coach is helping you, have them suggest some options based on what your trusted source said. Again, this is a brainstorm; the more options you can come up with, the better. Don't worry about whether they're accurate or not.

Choosing a Purpose Statement

Trusted sources often don't provide information about all three aspects of purpose at first, so don't worry if you only have enough information to make purpose statements in one or two of the categories. For example, it's common to receive essence and blessing information at first, but not to get mission information. No problem; just work with purpose statements in the essence and blessing areas.

Pick one of the three aspects and use the following process to converge on a "winner" from among the draft purpose statements you wrote.

1. Slowly read each one of your essence-based purpose statements out loud.

2. After you read each one out loud, rate it on a scale of 1 to 5 for the strength of the emotional or physical reaction you experience. The nature of the reaction does not matter, only the strength of it. It may be a positive or negative reaction.

3. After you have read all of the purpose statements out loud and rated each one for its impact on you—emotional or physical—pick out the one, two, or three purpose statements that have the highest rating.

4. If you have more than one purpose statement with a high rating, read each one out loud. If there is one to which you react less strongly than the others, eliminate it. If you have two that are different and both very strong, you do not need to choose among them. It is okay to have more than one purpose statement.

5. Now repeat the process for the next category: work with your blessing-based purpose statements. Repeat Steps 1-4 for your blessing-based purpose statements, until you have one or two "winners."

6. If you have mission information, repeat the process again for your mission-based purpose statements, until you have one or two to which you react most strongly.

7. Now go back and look through the purpose statements you didn't choose. Double-check to see if there is one you ignored because you really didn't like it. Really not liking a purpose statement is a sign of accuracy! Put it on the list with the other winners.

8. You're done! You should have roughly 1-5 purpose statements.

If you wish, you can try editing some of them a little bit. If you do, it is critical that you repeat the exercise of checking for a reaction. Each time you make a change to a purpose statement, read the old version and the new version out loud. If you don't get a stronger reaction from the new version, abandon the change and go back to the old version.

There is one final step before your purpose statements are complete. Go back and check with your trusted source! When your ego gets involved in creating purpose statements, you immediately run the risk that your ego will censor and edit them into something it likes. This usually degrades the potency of the purpose statement, wringing all of the juice and life out of it. It is extremely important to stick with the most impactful purpose statements, even if they make your skin crawl or if your inner Skeptic goes nuts when you say them.

Each purpose statement must be short, simple, and easy to remember. If you cannot remember it, you will not be able to use it when you are making decisions. Place these purpose statements in some prominent place where you will see them. If you are concerned about others seeing them, do it in such a way that you will not need to reveal or discuss them with other people. For now, these purpose statements are for your use and your use only.

Some people are bothered by having more than one purpose statement. They try to combine two or three together into one sentence. This invariably results in some unwieldy monstrosity that has lost all of its power. The better way to do this is to create a "purpose paragraph." Write all of your winning purpose statements down as individual sentences, one after another. Now read this entire paragraph slowly, out loud. If you carefully followed the instructions above, this should be pretty difficult to do, as you will probably have a very strong reaction when you do it.

Congratulations! You now have your purpose statement, or statements. You have achieved a very important milestone. Now you can skip ahead to Chapter 11: Living Your Purpose.

> *"We must not, in trying to think about how we can make a big difference, ignore the small daily differences we can make which, over time, add up to big differences that we often cannot foresee."*
>
> – Marian Wright Edelman

Chapter Ten

I Didn't Find My Purpose—What's Up?

What's Wrong?

Finding your purpose is essentially a communication exercise, a communication between your ego and your trusted source. As with any form of communication, it can break down in several places. For simplicity's sake, let's pretend that you're making a phone call to your trusted source. There are three things that can prevent a conversation from taking place: you (that is, your ego), the trusted source, and the phone equipment.

The most common communication breakdown happens on the ego side. This happens when one or more protective parts of your ego deem that it is unsafe, unwise, or unnecessary for you to have contact with your trusted source. Having decided this, it is very easy for the inner protectors to sabotage any effort you make to find your purpose. This is equivalent to you not making the call, not listening, or dialing the wrong number. The problem is on your side of the communication.

If you have been unable to make any kind of contact with your trusted source, the best thing is to go back and do the exercise "Negotiating with Inner Protectors" in Chapter 4: Clearing a Path through the Ego. You may have missed some part of you that objects to you knowing your purpose. And, without its permission, you will be unable to proceed and get information from your trusted source. Until all of the parts of your ego have decided that learning your purpose is a good idea, little will happen.

Another problem that occurs is when a person has very little experience of spiritual, religious, or psychological work. If you have never delved into the spiritual realm and never done any work on yourself internally, it may be difficult to establish a clear connection with your trusted source. This is equivalent to a problem with the phone line, like not knowing which number to call or having a problem with your phone service. You want to talk, but you can't get a line through. Any introspective practice will help with this, if this is in fact the problem. Therapy, meditation, consciousness workshops, and prayer will all increase your capacity to focus internally, which will make it easier to connect with your trusted source.

The third form of communication problem occurs on the trusted source's side. The trusted source is almost always willing to make some form of contact, although it may be unwilling to reveal certain information. I have experienced instances with clients where their trusted source flatly refused to reveal any information about their purpose. This happens when the trusted source deems that knowing your purpose would not support your growth and development. The trusted source may be concerned that the information would be too frightening for you and that knowing it would scare you into paralysis. It might also be concerned that if you have too much information, you might make choices that are not in support of your purpose. No matter how badly you want to find your purpose, your trusted source will wait patiently until it believes you are ready. For this reason, trusted sources are more likely to withhold purpose information from young people.

If you have made contact with your trusted source and your trusted source has refused to disclose information to you, all is not lost. I recommend that you go back, using the same method, and ask your trusted source what you should be doing to prepare to learn your purpose. You can still find out purposeful things you could do, even though you don't know your purpose. Usually, this will reveal some information that will help to make choices and move forward on your path. If you do have a direct connection working and don't know your purpose, you can still check in with your trusted source regularly to get advice and counsel on decisions that you're facing. This will establish a relationship that you can later use to learn your purpose when your trusted source deems the time to be right.

Here are some questions you can ask a trusted source that refuses to disclose information about your purpose:

- ✓ "Why won't you tell me about my purpose?"
- ✓ "What needs to change before I can learn my purpose?"
- ✓ "How can I make these changes?"
- ✓ "What should I focus on in the meantime?"

The answers to these questions will provide you with a direction and path forward. Following this path will allow you to live purposefully, even though you don't yet know your purpose. It will also lessen the amount of time it will take you to learn your purpose.

Living with Not Knowing

Having a strong desire to know your purpose and being unable to figure it out can be very frustrating. However, this is actually the state of many people in the world. It is a common and healthy way to go through life and there is no reason you should judge yourself for it. In fact, some people's trusted sources deem that their ability to be unattached to knowing their purpose is the best training they can get for manifesting their purpose. This can result in long periods of time when you desire to know your purpose and do not know it. For me, this period of time was 20 years. Hopefully it will be less for you. Seeking to move forward in your life gracefully and to identify your path as best you can is the best way to respond to this state of affairs.

Oddly, if you were able to establish contact with a trusted source and didn't find your purpose, you are in a much better place. Having a direct connection with a trusted source is more useful and more important than knowing your purpose. Yes, that's right, *more* useful and *more* important. People who know their purpose and don't maintain contact with their trusted source usually make very little progress. If you continue to consult your trusted source for advice on a regular basis, you can live a completely purposeful and fulfilling life without ever knowing your purpose. If you were unable to create a connection to a trusted source at all, yet still wish to walk your path, there is another method you can use.

Method 12: Pathfinding

Unlike all of the other methods, this method is not about finding out what your purpose is. This method is about using your intuitive capacities to make purposeful choices in the absence of knowing your purpose. I call it "pathfinding." It relies on your ability to detect certain telltale clues about which choices are and are not purposeful. Over time, this will help you move forward on your path and prepare you to know your purpose. I have met people who use this method consistently, live very much in the moment, and are completely happy and satisfied, even though they do not know their purpose. In some ways, this is the best method of all. All of the other methods are for those of us who are too impatient to live this way. This method relies on noticing two types of feedback as you move through your life:

1. External signs

2. Internal signs

Whether you know your purpose or not, behaving in a purposeful way elicits different responses than behaving in a non-purposeful way does. If you can learn to pay attention to the synchronistic signs around you, you can begin to see whether you are on or off purpose. If the chance coincidences in your environment are generally positive and supportive, this is an indication that you are on your path. If the chance coincidences in your environment are negative, this is a sign that you are off your path. This information can sometimes be difficult to interpret, but it is a skill you can learn if you practice it.

Pathfinding Exercise 1: External Signs

1. Remember a time recently when things were going well for you, when it seemed like you were firing on all cylinders and circumstances were conspiring to support you. What positive signs did you notice around you? Write them down. (Examples: people providing support and information just when you needed it, traffic lights all turning green, telephone call coming at just the right time) What were you doing, or trying to do, when this was happening?

2. Remember a time recently when things were going very badly for you, when it seemed like everything was going wrong and circumstances were conspiring to impede you. What negative signs did you notice around you? Write them down. (Examples: people failing to support you; unexpected obstacles, mistakes, and accidents; traffic lights all turning red; being unable to reach people with whom you needed to communicate) What were you doing, or trying to do, when this was happening?

Internal signs have to do with emotional and physical responses when making choices. Before I knew my purpose, people would frequently offer business opportunities to me. I could feel, in my body, a certain deflating sense, even though I didn't know my purpose. This was completely independent of my mind's idea of whether this was or was not a good idea. Something can seem like a good idea (i.e., make perfect sense to the ego) and not be purposeful. Usually, there is some physical or emotional response that quickens or enlivens when something is purposeful. Conversely, there is often a physical feeling of deflation or contraction when something is not purposeful. Learning to recognize these signs when making choices can also steer you in a purposeful direction.

When working with internal signs, the emotion of fear can be misleading. People often fear things that are purposeful for them, but it is an excited and overwhelmed kind of fear. Am I up to the challenge? Can I really be all of that? This is very different from the mind-numbing dread of contemplating another year at your dead-end job.

Pathfinding Exercise 2: Internal Signs

1. Remember a time recently when you were engaged in an activity that seemed effortless, exciting, and fulfilling. What positive signs and feelings did you notice inside yourself? Write them down. (Examples: passion, joy, losing track of time, more stamina than usual) What were you doing, or trying to do, when this was happening?

2. Remember a time recently when you were engaged in an activity that seemed difficult, unrewarding, and depressing. What negative signs and feelings did you notice inside yourself? Write them down. (Examples: boredom, resentment, fatigue, depression, sickness, being easily distracted) What were you doing, or trying to do, when this was happening?

These two exercises are backwards-looking; that is, they look at things that have already happened. Their purpose is to help you find and tune the mechanisms that you will use to make decisions. Pathfinding is most useful and interesting when it is applied to things that are happening right now or that haven't happened yet. Your ability to notice whether the thing you are doing right now is purposeful is very important, and your ability to apply your pathfinding radar to a decision about the future is critical.

Pathfinding Exercise 3: Making a Decision

Pick some choice that you're facing in your life. When you're learning this method, it's best to use some activity that you're contemplating doing. Examples: "Should I take the new job offer or stick with my current job?" "My colleague wants me to participate in a new work project. Should I?" "Which dance class should I take?"

1. Write down the question you're trying to answer.

2. Make a list of the various options you're being presented. It could be as simple as two options or it could be a whole list of options.

3. In order to clear your mind and get your ego out of the way, write down your ego's evaluation of each of the choices in the space provided. That is, write down whether you think this thing is a good or bad option and why.

4. Read the first option out loud. See if you can detect some sense of excitement and elation or, conversely, deflation and depression when you say the choice out loud. Pay attention to subtle emotional and physical cues. Write down what you feel and experience next to this option.

5. Repeat this process for each option, saying it out loud and writing down your physical and emotional response.

6. The option that generated the most positive physical and emotional energy is likely the most purposeful one. However, you do not need to choose this option. Weighing both your pathfinding response and your ego's thoughts and feelings about which makes the most sense, choose whichever option you wish.

7. When you actually do the activity, notice how it turns out.

You will need to practice this method to gain skill at noticing and interpreting your physical and emotional responses. This is not an exact science. If you practice this over time, you will become nearly constantly aware of your internal state as you go through life, and you'll be able to use that state to navigate your path. This is a tremendously powerful way to live.

I have found over time that my pathfinding sense, my physical and emotional responses, are a much better predictor of success than my mind's idea of what will work. See if you find the same!

Example

Buzz Sztukowski was a one-on-one coaching client, one of many successful, dissatisfied, high-level executives with whom I've worked. Here is how he describes the situation, as it was before we began to work on his purpose:

"I felt a lack of meaning and purpose in my life, particularly at work. I was making good money, but that just wasn't enough. I dedicated time and energy to work because I wanted to make a difference. Some of it was meaningful, but there wasn't much of me in it. Work took so much energy away from my family and hobbies. I was cynical about other people, especially when they disagreed with me. I quit my job because I was willing to try almost anything to make it different."

After going through the processes outlined in this book, we were not able to learn anything about his essence, blessing, or mission. In this case, Buzz's trusted source was unwilling to disclose any of the aspects of his purpose. Undaunted, Buzz was determined to live a purposeful life nonetheless. He established regular spiritual practices and paid close attention to which work and personal activities felt and did not feel purposeful to him. He particularly noticed when he was being brusque, cynical, and stressed and when he was being calm, joyful, and purposeful. Here is how Buzz describes his situation now, after a year of pathfinding:

"I still know nothing about my essence, blessing, and mission, but the world is so much more exciting and meaningful to me than it was. Through meditation, prayer, and focusing on who I'm being in my life, I've opened up doors into whole new parts of myself that I never knew were there. I look at my day as practice: I can use my old strengths (but not overuse them) and practice new ones. I'm much more relaxed now. I approach my day with meaning. It didn't happen overnight, but I can see a big difference as I look back. Although I can't tell you my purpose, I know that what I am doing is absolutely purposeful. When new opportunities arise, I can feel almost immediately whether they are purposeful for me. Instead of being cynical about people and judging them, I think more about their point of view and how I can influence them. At the end of the day, I know my day was purposeful, and that feels really good. I know I will keep growing and that the best is yet to come."

If you have been unable to learn any details about your purpose, you can still choose to live purposefully. Do you? If so, keep reading. In addition to Pathfinding, there are practices in the final chapter that you can do even if you don't have specific purpose information.

Chapter Eleven

Living Your Purpose

Now that you've created one or more purpose statements, let's talk about how to bring your purpose out into your life. As I mentioned earlier, simply knowing your purpose will have little impact. Achieving the fulfillment, success, and sense of meaning that most people desire depends on the changes you make in your life based on your purpose. As with every other decision that your ego faces, this is a choice. I often ask my executive coaching clients where they would like to place themselves on a scale from 1 to 10, where 1 is ignoring their purpose completely and 10 is making the remainder of their life about their purpose. This is a critical decision, so let's talk about it in detail.

Although it is uncommon, it is entirely legitimate to do absolutely nothing with your new understanding of your purpose. As I've articulated over and over again, choice is the domain of the ego, not the trusted source. Your ego has a very specific responsibility to make choices that it deems are safe for you and will bring you the most happiness. This might mean completely ignoring your purpose. This choice must be an option, because without it your ego really does not have free will. You must be willing to at least consider doing nothing about your purpose. In effect, this means going back to a life where you choose those things that your ego desires and make the best of them. This has positive and negative consequences, as does any choice.

Let's look at those consequences. On the upside, your ego may feel some pull in this direction if it fears your purpose or what might happen if you pursue your purpose. Choosing to ignore your purpose is usually a strategy for maintaining some sense of control over your life. This control is not as real as it might seem, because your unconscious and your trusted source will continue to influence your life. Steering away from or ignoring your purpose may cause your trusted source to engage in sabotaging behaviors. Nonetheless, living an ordinary life, ignorant of purpose, is an entirely legitimate and healthy choice.

At the other end of the spectrum, those who choose to express their purpose at a "10" are seeking to make their life a full expression of their purpose. While for many people this is the most frightening choice, it is also the most exhilarating and rewarding. Choosing fully in favor of purpose creates the most meaning, fulfillment, and, usually, the most success in a lifetime. People often choose this strategy when they're playing for the endgame, what I call the "deathbed experience." That is, when you are lying in your deathbed at the end of your life looking back, what do you want to remember?

I have friends and associates who have done hospice work with dying people. They assure me that very rarely do dying people worry about the choices they made. They are much more likely to worry about the choices they didn't make. Final regrets are usually about risks not taken, paths not walked, and efforts not made. Usually, at this stage, people are not concerned or upset about things they tried to do that failed, rather with things they didn't try to do.

Choosing 8-10 on a scale of 10 means making your life fully about purpose. This doesn't happen overnight; it is a process. There is little value in turning your life upside down in a single day, week, or month. For most people, making their life about purpose takes one to three years to implement. It is a process that can take a while to do in orderly fashion. Usually, this requires some form of qualified assistance, either general assistance from a coach or specific assistance at getting into a new field or endeavor that is more purposeful than the one you've been in. It does not necessarily mean that you have to change careers or professions, although it can mean that. What it does mean is that you must make most, if not all, aspects of your life an expression of your purpose in some way, shape, or form. It also means that you will need to express your purpose clearly to other people.

For many people, their goal is somewhere in between, say 5-7 on a scale of 10. Nearly any purpose can be expressed in a given job. It is usually possible to find some way to express your purpose in your work or life, no matter what you do. This usually means changing *how* you do what you do, not necessarily what you do. More importantly, it definitely entails changing *why* you do what you do. I sometimes refer to this way of operating as "stealth mode." It is stealth mode in the sense that you can perform your purpose without making it clear to others that that's what you're doing. For those who choose 8-10, it does not work to operate in stealth mode. People who choose a 10 must wear their purpose on their sleeve.

What is your choice? On a scale of 1-10, how purposeful do you desire to be in your life?

Making Purposeful Choices

If you choose to live your life purposefully, the rubber meets the road when you are facing decisions. Ultimately, how your life is impacted by your purpose will depend on the extent to which you refer to your purpose when making choices. For the most minor decisions, such as what to have for dinner or what clothes to wear, purpose may have no bearing. But for larger decisions, such as what kind of work to do, where to live, and what kind of relationships to have, purpose will have a strong bearing. You do not need to choose the most purposeful option in every decision, but the degree to which your life is improved by your purpose will depend on the number of times you choose in favor of purpose. Let's take an individual decision as an example.

Let's say that you are in the market for a new job and you have been extended two job offers. Your ego will no doubt have pros and cons associated with each of these choices, things like working hours, money, length of commute, prestige, and how you imagine you will feel while doing the work. To make a purposeful choice, you would consider your purpose while making your decision. You would also employ a direct access method to contact your trusted source and ask it for counsel regarding the choice. Bear in mind that your trusted source may not give you direct instructions; it may instead give you advice on how to choose. Your trusted source will often elect to train you rather than tell you what to do.

In the end, one of the choices will likely be more purposeful than the other. It may not be the same choice your ego favors. Remember that you are free to choose either way. But living your life purposefully requires that you make a series of decisions in favor of your purpose. Choosing in favor of your ego and against your purpose time after time will lead you away from meaning, purpose, and, ultimately, away from fulfillment and success. Life will once again become confusing and take on the gray tones of lack of passion. The best possible choices are those where you can find a sweet spot, an option where the desires of your ego and the advice of your trusted source and purpose intersect. These options are both purposeful for you and appealing and pleasing to your ego.

Viewing every decision as a simple "either/or" choice between your trusted source and your ego will only create inner conflict. Consistently choosing things that are purposeful but that your ego dislikes will cause fear. Your personal ego-needs will not be met. In the end, this is not sustainable because your ego protectors will rebel, take over, and steer you back into things that feel more safe, comfortable, and familiar.

Consistently choosing in favor of your ego against your purpose will slowly leach the meaning from your life. In the end, this choice will not be sustainable either, because it will lead to a humdrum grind of daily existence and, potentially, to depression and disease.

The other critical aspect of making purposeful choices is saying "no" to those things that are not purposeful. For many people, this can be very challenging. Clearing your to-do list and calendar of those things that have nothing to do with your purpose is one of the best ways to move forward on your path. If you're like most people, the profusion of non-purposeful things that accumulate in your day can distract you from the life you were meant to lead. They also anchor you in your current reality, preventing you from moving forward along your path. The willingness to release these things can accelerate your progress.

With all of this choice making, I want to advocate strongly for making sensible, rational choices that take purpose into account. As I said, turning your life upside down overnight will serve nothing. Things like changing professions, divorcing spouses, or moving are critical decisions that must be weighed carefully both in terms of purpose and in light of ego values and desires.

Remember that part of your ego's job is to keep you safe. Safety is a useful thing. If you decide that you have to change jobs or sever relationships with people who stand in the way of your purpose, it is very important that you do that in a responsible and respectful manner. I have never heard a trusted source tell someone to behave in a rude or dismissive fashion or to nonchalantly break agreements and commitments they have made. Remember, moving from the life you've had to a more purposeful one is a process. The rate at which you engage in this process is up to you.

Exercise: Make a Purposeful Choice

Pick a decision that you need to make soon. For practice, this exercise will work better with a medium-sized decision, something in between choosing what kind of bread you want on your sandwich and deciding whether to quit your job.

1. Write down the list of possible options you need to choose from.

2. For each option, write a list of pros and cons. What are the upside and downside of each choice? (This is your ego's chance to express its preferences.)

3. Now read your purpose. Your blessing and/or mission will probably be the most useful aspects of your purpose to use in this exercise. Rate each option on a scale of 1-5 for how well it aligns with your purpose.

4. Using whichever direct access method has worked for you, consult your trusted source. Ask it for advice and feedback on the situation. Ask which option is most purposeful.

5. Weighing all of the input and factors, make a decision. Remember, you do not have to choose the most purposeful option! You can do whatever you like. You just need to take your purpose into account.

Now, the most important part: Watch what happens! Do events play out the way you expected or hoped? Frequently, people find that going with the most purposeful option consistently turns out the best. You may need to try this exercise several times in order to test this for yourself.

In some situations, your purpose may not create a preference of one choice over another. Many times I have heard trusted sources refuse to pick from a list of options and encourage the person to make their own choice. Not a problem! Just pick an option and go forward.

The ego desperately wants there to be "right" and "wrong" decisions. For many people, this is a much more comfortable framework in which to operate. A world divided into right and wrong is simple and comforting. Trusted sources often push back against this perspective. Would you be willing to live in a reality in which there is no right and wrong, only choices and consequences? There is learning down every path. Which path do you prefer to take?

Synchronicity

The pioneering psychiatrist Carl Jung often used the term "synchronicity" when referring to events and circumstances that happen randomly but seem to have some greater meaning. Experiences of synchronicity are very common when you are engaged in a search for purpose or engaging in the process of transforming your life to a more purposeful one. Examples of synchronicity include chance meetings, support appearing from nowhere, and other things that seem to defy probability. Think of it like a "coincidence."

I encourage you to interpret synchronicity as a form of communication from your trusted source. As you make more and more purposeful choices, the degree of positive synchronicity occurring in your life will increase. This can be both exhilarating and frightening. It has the general effect of accelerating you forward along your path.

If you are consistently making purposeful choices, then this synchronicity should take the form of support: chance meetings and occurrences that move you towards your purpose. For example, when I worked diligently on getting this book published, leaders would call me out of the blue seeking my services or offering me speaking engagements with groups of CEOs. While in a purposeful state, I have had opportunities seemingly drop out of the sky, one after another. The ego can have difficulty grasping this apparently nonlinear, illogical way of moving through life. Trusted sources are able to arrange help and circumstances that can move things forward faster than any plan your ego is capable of creating. If you are consistently making choices in opposition to your purpose, then you can expect this synchronicity to take the form of obstacles and even sabotage. Think of Murphy's Law: Everything that can go wrong will go wrong.

These responses are predictable, so expect them. They are one of the ways that you can test the accuracy of your purpose. When clients of mine are strongly skeptical after having found their purpose, I encourage them to go out and make purposeful choices. I predict that they will experience positive synchronicity if they do so. This nearly always happens, much to the client's surprise. Conversely, you can test it by making non-purposeful choices and watching Murphy's Law go into effect.

Communicating Your Purpose to Others

When you first discover your purpose, it can be an exciting time. You may be so excited that you want to tell the whole world about it. Not so fast! I caution you to start with those people whom you trust deeply, the ones from whom you expect a positive and supportive response. Do not start with your boss, your grumpy and skeptical spouse, or your parent who always disapproves of everything you do. Go first to your trusted friend, your supportive relative, the friendly coworker with whom you share everything. You may not get a positive response from all of these people, but your odds are better!

As with anything else, you can expect a mix of responses from the world—both approval and disapproval. The prospect of this can be frightening, because being rejected at the level of purpose can cut deep. To some, it feels like a very personal rejection, a dismissal of who you are at the most fundamental level. If you are serious about living your purpose, sooner or later you will have to communicate it to others.

So what do you do if you get a bad reception? Treat it as a test. Are you serious about your purpose? Will you stick to your guns and move towards it even if not everyone in your life approves of it, or of you?

Which is more important to you, the approval of others or your reason for being? Bear in mind that as you move towards your purpose, some people will approve of you more. Be careful whose approval you seek!

If you choose to live a fully purposeful life, speaking about your purpose will become a regular habit. Think of it as if you are wearing your purpose on your sleeve, tattooing it on your forehead, or putting it on your business card. You may not describe your purpose in exactly the way you communicate it to yourself. Private purpose statements often have a spiritual component or references to specific terms that don't make sense to the general public. For this reason, it may make sense to create a version of your purpose statement that can be understood by someone without a lot of explanation. This is especially important for service professionals, for whom communicating their purpose can directly affect how they market themselves. It is also critically important for leaders communicating their vision.

The aspects of purpose that are most relevant here are blessing and mission. These are the aspects of your purpose that are about action, about doing. Think of your purpose statement(s). What is it they ask you to do? For whom do they ask you to do it? These are classical marketing questions. Typical marketing strategy would ask you to come up with a service or product that is desired by the market. This is usually done by looking for a new niche, some need that is not being fulfilled. At the level of purpose, this is absolutely the wrong approach. Instead, come up with a product or service that is a direct expression of your purpose. Market or sell that product or service to those people who are the natural target audience for your blessing and/or mission.

In order to do this, you will need to reframe your purpose statement in terms that will be understandable to your target market. This is where classical marketing tells you to do exactly the right thing. Check with people in your target market, those whom you have been sent to serve. (If you don't know who they are, go ask your trusted source!) Find out whether your blessing makes sense to them. Would they want to hire you? If your blessing makes sense, it will be compelling to people in your target market. If not, you will need to find another way to say it when you talk about it publicly.

Exercise: Test Your Purpose Statement for Public Use

In marketing, a short pithy statement that tells someone who you are or what you do is referred to as an "elevator pitch." The idea is that you can explain yourself to someone quickly, before the elevator gets to their floor and they leave. Your purpose statement may make a fabulous elevator pitch, if the people you've been sent to serve can understand it easily.

1. Write down all of your purpose statements, exactly as you created them when you did the purpose statement exercise.

2. To get the most benefit from this exercise, you will need the help of someone whom you've been sent to serve. For example, if your trusted source told you that you have been sent to help troubled teens, get some help from a troubled teen. If your mission is to work with business leaders, get a CEO friend on the phone.

3. If you can't get help from someone you've been sent to serve, get a friend or colleague to pretend they're in that group. For example, ask your friend to imagine that she is a troubled teen or to pretend that she is a CEO. The worst thing you can do is to do this exercise by yourself. Your ego is too likely to play tricks on you.

4. Read your blessing-based purpose statement(s) out loud to your "client."

5. Ask for feedback. Is it compelling to them? Confusing? Does it inspire curiosity? Curiosity and interest are good; confusion and bafflement are bad. Lack of a reaction is bad as well.

If your blessing-based purpose statement inspires curiosity and interest, it may be ready for prime time. You may feel nervous about talking about your purpose in public; that's fine. Expressing your purpose accurately can be a very vulnerable thing. It is precisely that vulnerability that can make it so compelling to those you've been sent to serve. Try it and see what happens!

If your "sample client" can't understand what you're talking about, then you need a "public use" purpose statement. This is a translation of your purpose statement that has the same meaning, but is comprehensible in everyday language.

Exercise: Create a Purposeful Marketing Statement

You only need to do this exercise if your blessing-based purpose statement is confusing to the people you've been sent to serve. If your blessing generates interest and curiosity in your "target market," skip this exercise and go with it as is!

In this exercise, your ego's natural tendency to edit and censor your purpose statement will probably come up. There are two ways to translate your purpose statement for public use. The natural and most common way is to make it bland and generic so that no one could find it objectionable. This is a fear-based approach and will leach all of the life from your purpose statement.

The more effective way is to translate your blessing-based purpose statement into common, everyday language while leaving its basic meaning completely intact. This may mean that it will confront or exclude certain people for whom your purpose is not appropriate. While the ego desires to be accepted by everyone, this is not, in fact, useful. If people hear the public version of your purpose statement and deem that what you do is not appropriate for them, this is a good thing. Remember that moving forward on your purpose means saying "no" to things that are not purposeful. This includes saying "no" to jobs, clients, and customers for whom your purpose is not appropriate. Therefore, your public purpose statement should be a simple and clear articulation of what you do and who you do it for, in the most purposeful terms possible.

1. Re-read what your trusted source said about your blessing.

2. Using words taken directly from your trusted source, brainstorm a list of different ways you can describe what you do when you're doing your blessing.

3. Using words taken directly from your trusted source, brainstorm a list of different ways to describe the people for whom you do this.

4. Now try different combinations of the two lists to come up with simple statements that describe what you do and for whom you do it.

5. Using the helper you engaged in the previous exercise, read each statement out loud. See which statements cause a curious, interested reaction.

The resulting statement should be simple, direct, and easy to remember. It will probably also make you somewhat uncomfortable to imagine saying it out loud to people. This is actually a good sign. Here are some examples of what the result might look like:

✓ "I help leaders who are meant to change the world find their way."

✓ "I awaken middle-aged women who have lost their passion."

✓ "I help messengers spread their message to the world."

✓ "I help visionary leaders who ache heal themselves and bring their gifts to the world."

Michael Port, author of *Book Yourself Solid*, calls this a "who and do what" statement. Michael's system is designed to help you turn your life's purpose into a business that makes you money. If you are concerned about how to do this, I strongly recommend that you check out his books and programs.

Ongoing Dialogue with Your Trusted Source

If you choose to live your life purposefully, it is very important that you use some direct access method to communicate with your trusted source on a regular basis. This could be daily, weekly, or even monthly, but some regularity is required. This ongoing communication will support you in several ways. First, as with any muscle, the more you use your ability to connect with your trusted source, the stronger it will become. Think of this as widening a pipe, allowing more water to flow through it. Or, for you techno geeks, increasing the bandwidth of your connection.

Secondly, it will allow you to get regular information and updates about your progress along your path. As you move forward, your understanding of your purpose statement may change because more information may become available from your trusted source. Or, your purpose may ask you to move in a new direction. What is purposeful at one phase of your life may not be purposeful at another phase.

The ego can often tend to move in a straight line without regard for turns in the road. Once you're doing something that works, your ego may imagine that if you just keep doing it, everything will stay great. But remember that your trusted source wants you to learn and grow, and this requires change. Once this phase of your life is complete, your trusted source will guide you to something new. If your ego resists this turn in the road, you may find yourself going straight. First comes the feeling of scraping against the guardrail, then hitting the embankment, perhaps eventually wrapping yourself around a metaphorical "tree." I have experienced more than one of these "car wrecks" in my life, and they are no fun. Staying in touch with your trusted source can prevent this, keeping you apprised of the turns in the road as they come.

Lastly, ongoing communication with your trusted source will have a subtle but pervasive effect on your ordinary, everyday state of consciousness. When your sense of self is restricted to your ego, you may become little more than a basket of fears and needs. Having a sense of partnership with your trusted source allows you to expand your sense of identity and see yourself as the far more capable and much vaster being you truly are.

Establish a regular practice for yourself. Check in with your trusted source and ask simple, open-ended questions about events that are going on in your life. Get advice and counsel about how to proceed. Also, if there are questions about your purpose that were not answered, you may go back and ask them again. If you have been resolute in following the instructions your trusted source gave you and have behaved in a purposeful manner, more information should become available over time.

The Greatest Gift

You may recall something I said much earlier in this book, that most of us are being driven in our life by the fear and pain of our original sacred wound. This is at the root of your ego's desire to control life, to avoid pain and struggle, to manage how others perceive you, and to judge and categorize everyone and everything.

My goal in this book has been to help you shift from this wound-driven, ego-driven state to a larger, purpose-driven state. My wish for you is that when you say "I," the "I" you speak of is larger than it once was. Making purposeful choices and communicating with your trusted source will help with this over time, but there is one more thing you can do.

To help your psyche make the transition into this expanded state of being, you must *give your blessing to yourself*. If you have been sent into the world to give love to the wounded, then first you must give love to yourself. If you have been sent to help people find their path, then first you must find your own path. If you have been sent to show people their true selves, then first you must see your true self. If you have been sent to heal those who have lost hope, then first you must heal yourself.

You are a magnificent gift, sent by your trusted source to all of the people of the world. The world desperately needs what you have brought. But don't forget that you are one of the people of the world. You are a gift sent to yourself, as well. We have been waiting for you for a long time, but we can wait just a little bit longer, while you give this gift to yourself first. We'll get in line, right behind you.

Appendix:

Resources

CLEARING A PATH THROUGH THE EGO

The methods listed here can only be used for clearing a path through the ego. Additional methods listed below, under Access to Purpose, can also be used for clearing a path through the ego.

Emotional Freedom Technique (EFT)

EFT
PO Box 269
Coulterville, CA 95311
www.emofree.com

Eye Movement Desensitization and Reprocessing (EMDR)

EMDR Institute, Inc.
PO Box 750
Watsonville, CA 95077
Phone: (831) 761-1040
Fax: (831) 761-1204
Email: inst@emdr.com
www.emdr.com

Lefkoe Method

The Lefkoe Institute
180 Forrest Avenue
Fairfax, CA 94930-1805
Toll Free: (866) 533-5631
Phone: (415) 456-7300
Fax: (415) 485-3865
Email: info@lefkoeinstitute.com
www.lefkoeinstitute.com

Sedona Method

Sedona Training Associates
60 Tortilla Drive
Sedona, AZ 86336
Toll Free: (888) 282-5656
Phone: (928) 282-3522
www.sedona.com

Tapas Acupressure Technique (TAT)

TATLife
PO Box 5192
Mooresville, NC 28117
Toll Free: (877) 674-4344
Phone: (310) 378-7381
www.tatlife.net

ACCESS TO PURPOSE

Purpose Programs

I offer workshops and teleseminars for finding your life's purpose through my online community:

www.truepurposecommunity.com

Essence Conversation

The Accomplishment Coaching school teaches an ingenious indirect method for identifying essence, called the Essence Conversation.

Accomplishment Coaching
964 Fifth Avenue, Suite 506
San Diego, CA 92101
Toll Free: (888) 548-6813
Phone: (619) 238-3600
Email: ContactUs@accomplishmentcoaching.com
www.accomplishmentcoaching.com

Active Imagination

Active imagination can be used for clearing a path through the ego and for connecting to a trusted source.

Inner Work: Using Dreams and Active Imagination for Personal Growth
by Robert Johnson (1989)

Dream Work

The International Association for the Study of Dreams
www.asdreams.org

Jeremy Taylor
The Marin Institute for Projective Dream Work
www.jeremytaylor.com

Bob and Hilary Beban
Exploring Dreams
www.exploringdreams.com

Inner Work: Using Dreams and Active Imagination for Personal Growth
by Robert Johnson (1989)

Dream Work by Jeremy Taylor (1983)

Man and His Symbols by C.G. Jung, et. al. (1968)

Gestalt Therapy

Gestalt therapy can be used for clearing a path through the ego and for connecting to a trusted source.

The Gestalt Therapy Network
www.gestalttherapy.net

Hypnotherapy

Hypnotherapy can be used for clearing a path through the ego and for connecting to a trusted source. There are many schools and organizations devoted to the practice and training of hypnotherapy. These are but a few.

Hypnotherapy Training Institute
4730 Alta Vista Avenue
Santa Rosa, CA 95404
Toll Free: (800) 256-6448
Phone: (707) 579-9023
www.hypnotherapy.com

American Council of Hypnotist Examiners
700 S. Central Avenue
Glendale, CA 91204
Phone: (818) 242-1159
Fax: (818) 247-9379
Email: hypnotismla@earthlink.net
www.hypnotistexaminers.org

The American Board of Hypnotherapy
4224 Waialae Avenue, Suite 347
Honolulu, HI 96816
Toll Free: (888) 823-4823
www.abh-abnlp.com

Hypnosis Motivation Institute
18607 Ventura Boulevard, Suite 310
Tarzana, CA 91356-4158
Toll Free: (800) 479-9464
Phone: (818) 758-2747
Fax: (818) 344-2262
www.hypnosis.edu

Internal Family Systems Therapy (IFS)

IFS can be used for clearing a path through the ego and for connecting to a trusted source.

The Center for Self Leadership
PO Box 3969
Oak Park, IL 60303
Phone: (708) 383-2659
Fax: (708) 383-2399
Email: info@selfleadership.org
www.selfleadership.org

There are many IFS trainers and practitioners. I include the one below because he uses IFS for gaining permission from the ego as part of a life purpose process:

Jay Earley, Ph.D.
Phone: (415) 339-8060
Email: jay@LifePurposeCoaching.com
www.LifePurposeCoaching.com

Journey Work

Journey work can be used for clearing a path through the ego and for connecting to a trusted source.

The Foundation for Shamanic Studies
www.shamanism.org

Richard Whiteley
The Corporate Shaman (for leaders only)
www.corpshaman.com

Neuro-Linguistic Programming (NLP)

NLP can be used for clearing a path through the ego and for connecting to a trusted source. There are many schools and organizations devoted to the practice and training of NLP. These are but a few.

The American Board of NLP
4224 Waialae Avenue, Suite 347
Honolulu, HI 96816
Toll Free: (888) 823-4823
www.abh-abnlp.com

The NLP & Coaching Institute of California
Toll Free: (800) 767-6756
Phone: (801) 277-2014
www.nlpca.com

NLP Comprehensive
PO Box 648
Indian Hills, CO 80454-0648
Toll Free: (800) 233-1657
Phone: (303) 987-2224
Fax: (303) 987-2228
www.nlpco.com

NLP University
PO Box 1112
Ben Lomond, CA 95005
Phone: (831) 336-3457
Fax: (831) 336-5854
www.nlpu.com

Southern Institute of NLP
PO Box 529
Indian Rocks Beach, FL 33785
Phone: (813) 596-4891
Fax: (813)595-0040
www.intl-nlp.com

Retter Center
Yodfat
D.N. Misgav 20180
Israel
www.retter.co.il

Voice Dialogue

Voice Dialogue can be used for clearing a path through the ego and for connecting to a trusted source.

Drs. Hal and Sidra Stone
www.delos-inc.com

You can find other teachers on the "trainings by others" section of their website.

MANIFESTING YOUR PURPOSE

If you would like your newfound purpose to take root in your life, you have some work to do. I offer a program for manifesting your purpose through my online community:

www.truepurposecommunity.com

Marcia Wieder's Dream University has excellent programs for manifesting your purpose:

Marcia Wieder
Dream Coach, Inc.
110 Pacific Avenue, Suite 355
San Francisco, CA 94111
Phone: (415) 381-5564
Email: info@dreamcoach.com
www.dreamuniversity.com
And her book:
Making Your Dreams Come True (1999)

Michael Port has excellent methods for marketing your purpose-based business or practice:

Michael Port
Book Yourself Solid (2006)
www.bookyourselfsolid.com

Elizabeth Marshall's purpose is to "help messengers spread their message." Are you a messenger? Perhaps Elizabeth can help you:

Elizabeth Marshall
Marketing Coach and Strategist for Authors and Thought Leaders
5600 West Lovers Lane
Suite 116, PMB 142
Dallas, TX 75209
Phone: (214) 358-0567
Email: questions@marketingmarshall.com
www.marketingmarshall.com

Brookes is great at turning out an amazing book quickly! If your purpose calls you to create a book, Brookes is a solid resource who can assist you in making your vision a reality.

Brookes Nohlgren
Writer, Editor, & Book Producer
Helping You Create Books That Change Our World
Phone: (818) 783-0848
Email: brookes@booksbybrookes.com
www.booksbybrookes.com

Ann has a process for creating a book manuscript in a couple of days (really!). I created the first draft of this book in an afternoon using her methods.

Ann McIndoo
www.soyouwanttowrite.com

FINDING OTHER PEOPLE'S PURPOSE

I offer programs for coaches, consultants, therapists, counselors, pastors, and other professionals to train and certify them in finding their clients' purpose. I also teach professionals how to use their purpose to market themselves powerfully. You can learn about these programs by joining the Purposeful Coach Community:

www.purposefulcoach.com

Index

Lefkoe Method, a resource for clearing a
path through the ego, 68, 194
Life-change, xv–xviii
Life experiences, your soul "arranging"
for you, 27
Life purpose coaches, 26, 114
Life's purpose
defining, 1–15
the ego, 5–9
search for, 3–5
the soul, 12–15
step-by-step process for discovering, xv
the unconscious, 9–12
Likes and dislikes, 5
Listening
to the inner voice, 14–15
to the parts within, 122
for the response to prayer, 84
to the trusted source, 82
Living your purpose, 177–191
communicating your purpose to others,
184–189
the greatest gift, 190–191
making purposeful choices, 179–183
ongoing dialogue with your trusted
source, 189–190
synchronicity, 183–184

Manifesting your purpose, resources for,
199–200
Maslow, Abraham, 8
Meaning
assigned to happenings by the ego, 6–7
of life, 2–5, 31, 34
Medicine journeys, 40, 132–138
Meditation (Method 4), 92–98, 113–114.
See also Guided meditation
example, 95–97
exercises, 93–95
The methods, xx–xxii
#1: Purpose Hunting™, 27–37
#2: the Essence Conversation, 37–38
#3: prayer, 84–91
#4: meditation, 92–97
#5: journaling, 98–108
#6: dreaming, 108–112
#7: Voice Dialogue, 68, 114–122
#8: guided meditation, 123–125
#9: hypnotherapy, 126–127
#10: dream work, 127–131
#11: journey work, 132–138
#12: "pathfinding," 170–175

Mission
a component of purpose, 21–23
in purpose information, 155
sample purpose statements for, 159,
164
Money, 1, 45–46, 106
Murphy's Law, 184

Negotiation with inner protectors, 56–68
examples, 57–63
exercises, 64–67, 84
as Phase IV in getting permission from
the parts, 66
Neuro-linguistic programming (NLP),
a resource for accessing purpose, 68,
115, 198
New Year's resolutions, 8–9
NLP. *See* Neuro-linguistic programming
Not knowing, living with, 169–170

Oversimplified techniques, warning
about, 68–69
Overwhelm, 150

"**P**arts," 47. *See also* Permission from the
parts
"Passion," 30–31
Past life regression, 126
"Pathfinding" (Method 12), 170–175. *See
also* Clearing a path through the ego;
Steering you along your path
examples, 174–175
exercises, 171–174
when failing to find purpose, 170–175
Patterns. *See also* Speech patterns
in behavior, 33
of being, 33
of feeling, 33
sifting through, 33
symbolic, 33–34
Perfectionism, 52
Permission from the parts, securing,
64–67, 94, 96
Personal trusted sources, 76–78
Plant medicine guides, 134–135, 137
Prayer (Method 3), 84–91
examples, 86–91
exercise, 85–86
waiting for a response, 84
The Protector (or Controller, or Risk

About the Author

Tim Kelley is a nationally renowned expert on helping people find their life's purpose. He has worked with over a hundred CEOs and trained more than a thousand coaches, therapists, and consultants. He formerly worked as a leader at Oracle, two levels below the CEO. Tim has transformed entire organizations, coaching top leaders and executive teams from such companies as Nabisco, AOL, ING, Oracle, Lexmark, and Louis Dreyfus.

Tim's methods have been featured nationally in magazines and on TV. He has led trainings and workshops for over fifteen years in leadership, meditation, Voice Dialogue, and men's work, and he is certified by Helen Palmer to teach the *Enneagram*. Tim is also the co-author of *Wake Up... Live the Life You Love: Living on Purpose*, *A Search for Purpose*, and *Blueprint for Success*.

Tim has commanded military organizations, including an amphibious assault craft unit, and is a retired Naval Reserve officer. He holds a bachelor's degree in mathematics from MIT, where he taught calculus and studied philosophy and astronomy. He lives in Berkeley, California, with his wife and son.

www.TruePurposeBook.com